Conscience Warriors™
Never Give Up.
They Rise Up and Stand Strong.

Amen, amen, I say to you, no one can enter the kingdom of God without being born of water and Spirit. What is born of flesh is flesh and what is born of Spirit is spirit. Do not be amazed that I told you, 'You must be born from above'.
—John 3: 5-7
The New American Bible 1987

But when he comes, the Spirit of truth, he will guide you to all truth.
—John 16:13
The New American Bible 1987

CONSCIENCE WARRIORS™

UNITE WITH
THE HOLY SPIRIT IN TRUTH

BORN AGAIN FROM ABOVE

ANTHONY R. SOUZA

Published by:

SOUZA®

THE SOUZA AGENCY

ANNAPOLIS   MARYLAND

BORN AGAIN FROM ABOVE

UNITE WITH
THE HOLY SPIRIT IN TRUTH

Conscience Warriors

Are Completely Committed to
The Wonders of
God's Paschal Mystery as
Consubstantial which includes
Jesus' Hypostatic Union as
Perfectly, Simultaneously, and
Continuously Human & Divine that
Reveals and Demonstrates the
Salvation Pathway; also, that on
Pentecost, Jesus sent the Holy Spirit to
All of Mankind as a Faithful Gift
Always Available, as Counselor, in the
Personal Conscience.

Reference: *Encyclopedia of Catholicism*, HarperCollins Publishers 1995, 961

CONSCIENCE WARRIORS™
BORN AGAIN FROM ABOVE
UNITE WITH THE HOLY SPIRIT IN TRUTH

ANTHONY R. SOUZA, M.T.S.
Master of Theological Studies
Pontifical Lateran University in Rome
John Paul II Institute for Studies on Marriage and Family
   at the Catholic University of America

Published by: The Souza Agency, Inc.
Design by: Roseanne S. Souza
ConscienceWarriors.org
PO Box 128, Annapolis, MD 21404-0128
Library of Congress Control Number: 2025942542
ISBN: 978-0-9976297-8-1

DEDICATION

Conscience Warriors,
Born Again From Above,
is dedicated to my
Wonderful, Loving, and Blessed Sons,
Anthony Raymond Souza II, M.Ed.
&
Dominic Joseph Souza, Esq.

The Loving and Powerful Spirit of Brothers
Best Friends • Teammates
Leaders • Winners • Champions

As Sons, Loving Husbands, and Awesome
Fathers to our Seven Grandsons—
Gabriel, Nicholas, Nathaniel, Blake,
Vincent, Thomas, and Graham—
Tony and Dominic
are shining examples for others
in carrying out God's Plan of Generations
with utter Faithfulness and Devotion.

We thank God for gifting them to us
every moment of every day.

Tony and Dominic are profoundly,
deeply loved, and cherished by all of us.

✝

The Holy Spirit
Divine Counselor

Spirit of Truth
Spirit of Love
Spirit of Peace

Conscience Warriors
Born Again From Above

Table of Contents

Conscience Warriors, Born Again From Above

All believers in Christ, therefore, following the example of the Apostles, must fervently strive to conform their thinking and action to the will of the Holy Spirit...[1]

For only the Holy Spirit "convinces concerning sin," concerning evil, in order to restore what is good in man and in the world...[2]

THAT WHICH THE SPIRIT WILLS

A Conscience Warrior's quest is to be Born Again From Above and always be United with the Holy Spirit in Truth.

A Conscience Warrior's Faithful and successful pathway to Salvation is attainable with the personal embrace and engagement of the Holy Spirit.

1. Saint Pope John Paul II, *Dominum et Vivificantem*, Pauline Books & Media 1986, 111
2. Ibid., 123

TABLE OF CONTENTS
CONSCIENCE WARRIORS, BORN AGAIN FROM ABOVE

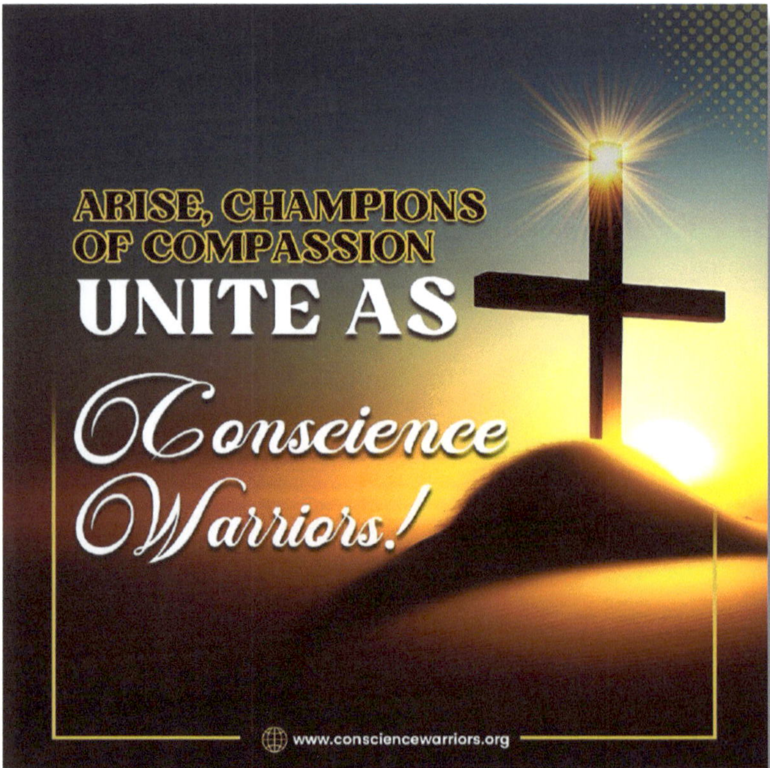
ARISE, CHAMPIONS
OF COMPASSION
UNITE AS
Conscience
Warriors!
www.consciencewarriors.org

RISE UP ALL MEN & WOMEN OF FAITH

FAITH

—— INTRODUCTION ——

BORN AGAIN FROM ABOVE

To assist all of us with further understanding of the Divine gift of our personal consciences, let us think for a few moments about the experience of Saint Nicodemus concerning his private evening meeting with Jesus Christ.

> *Now there was a Pharisee named Nicodemus,*
> *a ruler of the Jews. He came to Jesus at night*
> *and said to him, "Rabbi, we know that you are a*
> *teacher who has come from God, for no one can do*
> *these signs that you are doing unless God is with him."*
> *Jesus answered and said to him, "Amen, amen,*
> *I say to you, no one can see the kingdom of God*
> *without being born from above."*
> —John 3:1-3
> The New American Bible 1987

Nicodemus, a rich and religious man, was led by the truth to go to Jesus at night. Jesus was aware of Nicodemus' good faith efforts and schooled him on being Born Again.

Do not be amazed that I told you, 'You must be born from above.' The wind blows where it wills, and you can hear the sound it makes, but you do not know where it comes from or where it goes; so it is with everyone who is born of the Spirit."

—John 3:7-8
The New American Bible 1987

Schooled directly by Jesus about the pathway to Salvation, Nicodemus was then able to integrate his heart, mind, and conscience to synthesize the intellectual integrity that he desperately needed to successfully proceed on his spiritual journey for Salvation.

Nicodemus became Born Again in the image and likeness of Jesus Christ by embracing truth and breaking out and away from the "Go Along to Get Along" prevailing paradigm of the leaders of his times.

As we begin the journey of being **Born Again From Above,** let us always remember that Jesus, consubstantial with the Father and on Pentecost sent the Holy Spirit to be with all of us—the Counselor in our personal consciences—as a spiritual and Divine guide for our Salvation, United with the Holy Spirit in Truth.

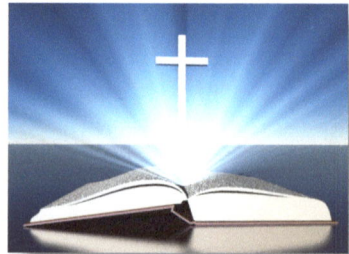

Anthony R. Souza, M.T.S.
Master of Theological Studies
Pontifical Lateran University in Rome
John Paul II Institute for Studies on Marriage and Family, at the Catholic University of America

— **I** —

JOSEPH OF ARIMATHEA
THE VERY FIRST
CONSCIENCE WARRIOR

WHO WAS JOSEPH OF ARIMATHEA?

✝ *Joseph of Arimathea, a distinguished member of the council, who was himself awaiting the kingdom of God, came and courageously went to Pilate and asked for the body of Jesus. Pilate was amazed that he was already dead. He summoned the centurion and asked him if Jesus had already died. And when he learned of it from the centurion, he gave the body to Joseph. Having bought a linen cloth, he took him down, wrapped him in the linen cloth and laid him in a tomb that had been hewn out of the rock. Then he rolled a stone against the entrance to the tomb.*
—Mark 15:43-46
The New American Bible 1987

Joseph of Arimathea is the world's first Conscience Warrior. Joseph loved Jesus Christ, our Savior, and was a secret follower of Jesus. He "broke out" from Collective Split-Conscience connected to the false teachings of the leaders of his time even though he feared them.

WHAT IS COLLECTIVE SPLIT-CONSCIENCE?

Collective Split-Conscience exists when two or more people work together to split their love using the disintegration of words and Faith-filled actions. The "Go Along to Get Along" paradigm is the source of energy and commitment for such nefarious collective action. This powers the aiding and abetting of those advocating grave sins like abortion, infanticide, child sexual abuse, gay marriage, transgenderism, false cultural division of systemic racism, Wokeism and its cancel culture, critical race and gender theories, and so much more. If one participates silently or actively in Collective Split-Conscience it can grow into one's Branded and Seared Conscience which can be fatal to the soul.

> **✝ Now the Spirit explicitly says that in the last times some will turn away from the faith by paying attention to deceitful spirits and demonic instructions through the hypocrisy of liars with branded consciences.**
> —1 Timothy 4:1-2
> The New American Bible 1987

WE ALL CAN BREAK OUT FROM COLLECTIVE SPLIT-CONSCIENCE

Joseph's actions to courageously and successfully "break out" and away from Collective Split-Conscience—of the religious leadership of his times—demonstrates the first and corrective step that the Salvation pathway demands!

Joseph of Arimathea put his words and actions together. He integrated them and avoided a Split-Conscience as well as the deadly Branded/Seared Conscience. Joseph has been venerated as a Saint and provides a living example for others to faithfully follow.

Today, we can follow Joseph of Arimathea's example like Nicodemus did—although a Pharisee and member of the Sanhedrin, he has also been venerated as a Saint—when he helped Joseph with Jesus' burial. You too can become a Conscience Warrior in today's times; or, drown in fear and self-focus while solely pursuing money, power, and glory.

Conscience Warriors follow in Joseph's and Nicodemus' footsteps. We reject the "groupthink" embedded in Collective Split-Conscience that pushes Wokeism and its related Atheism and Satanism to replace God. This includes the utter abuse of our precious and innocent children.

We work tirelessly to be filled with the integration of the truth and abundant love, and always Unite with The Holy Spirit in Truth. Join us.

Conscience Warriors go into the heat of the truth battle when today's Woke culture puts their Faith on the line.

Jesus knows what the Pharisees are thinking and He said to them:

Whoever is not with me is against me, and whoever does not gather with me scatters. Therefore, I say to you, every sin and blasphemy will be forgiven people, but blasphemy against the Spirit will not be forgiven. And whoever speaks a word against the Son of Man will be forgiven; but whoever speaks against the Holy Spirit will not be forgiven, either in this age or in the age to come.
—Matthew 12:30-32
The New American Bible 1987

The Holy Spirit—Divine Counselor, Spirit of Truth, Spirit of Love, Spirit of Peace—is always available to light up the Christian Faithful for navigating a successful pathway through the narrow gate.

The Advocate, the Holy Spirit that the Father will send in my name, he will teach you everything and remind you of all that I told you.
—John 15:26
The New American Bible 1987

Enter through the narrow gate; for the gate is wide and the road broad that leads to destruction, and those who enter through it are many. How narrow the gate and constricted the road that leads to life. And those who find it are few.
—Matthew 7:13-14

As Jesus said to Simon: Do not be afraid...
—Luke 5:10

Put out into deep water and lower your nets for a catch.
—Luke 5:4
The New American Bible 1987

— **II** —

JESUS SCHOOLS NICODEMUS THAT HE MUST BE BORN AGAIN TO BE SAVED

Nicodemus, a rich and religious man, was led by the truth to go to Jesus at night. He knew that Jesus had come from God because of the miracles that Jesus performed. Nicodemus believed his eyes and ears. Jesus was aware of Nicodemus' good faith efforts and schooled him on being Born Again.

NICODEMUS INTEGRATES HIS HEART, MIND, AND CONSCIENCE

Now there was a Pharisee named Nicodemus, a ruler of the Jews. He came to Jesus at night and said to him, "Rabbi, we know that you are a teacher who has come from God, for no one can do these signs that you are doing unless God is with him." Jesus answered and said to him, "Amen, amen, I say to you, no one can see the kingdom of God without being born from above."

—John 3:1-3
The New American Bible 1987

19

✝ *"Do not be amazed that I told you, 'You must be born from above.' The wind blows where it wills, and you can hear the sound it makes, but you do not know where it comes from or where it goes; so it is with everyone who is born of the Spirit."*
—John 3:7-8
The New American Bible 1987

Schooled directly by Jesus about the pathway to Salvation, Nicodemus was then able to integrate his heart, mind, and conscience to synthesize the intellectual integrity that he desperately needed to successfully proceed on his spiritual journey and fight bravely against a branded/seared conscience.

After he met and spoke with Jesus, Nicodemus became Born Again. In other words, Nicodemus—irrespective of hiding his true beliefs from the Pharisees and the Sanhedrin to avoid persecution and violence—became the first **Born Again** Conscience Warrior by breaking out from the "Go Along to Get Along" prevailing paradigm of the leaders of his time as he followed the footsteps of the world's First Conscience Warrior, Joseph of Arimathea.

WHOEVER LIVES THE TRUTH COMES TO THE LIGHT

Catholics and all Christians need to be **Born Again From Above**, to be spiritually re-born in the image and likeness of Jesus Christ. Salvation demands that we carry out the living example of Jesus in our daily lives. Pentecost delivers the Divine help of the Holy Spirit as Counselor in the human conscience. The human conscience must be filled with the Holy Spirit, God Himself, as the King of conscience and cannot be squeezed out by many in Church leadership that replace the Holy Spirit with Church pastors. Jesus was clear about the true meaning of **Born Again**.

What is born of flesh is flesh and what is born of the
Spirit is spirit. Do not be amazed that I told you,
'You must be born from above.'
—John 3:6-7
The New American Bible 1987

✝

And this is the verdict, that the light came into the world,
but people preferred darkness to light, because their
works were evil. For everyone who does wicked things
hates the light and does not come toward the light,
so that his works might not be exposed.
But whoever lives the truth comes to the light,
so that his works may be clearly seen as done in God.
—John 3:19-21
The New American Bible 1987

Being Born Again has nothing to do with the pastor-assisted "creative" to the "ideal" conscience which generates the needed false teaching to power "situation ethics" that justify "self-styled" Catholics. This pushing aside and keeping out the Holy Spirit in the personal conscience provides the sought after personal comfort and confidence for the person seeking "self-styled" religion. This further empowers the "Go Along to Get Along" personal paradigm of "situation ethics".

THE CHURCH MUST STOP
MISLEADING THE FAITHFUL

Currently in the world and very unfortunately, this unholy and solely human collaboration driven by "pastoral solutions"—that exclude the Holy Spirit's voice as Counselor, in the human conscience—is taking place routinely. Further, nefarious hypocrites and money changers throughout the world today are feeding off of Radical Feminism and its Immoral Slippery Slope. They help promote and accelerate the rapid growth of the "Go Along to Get Along" personal paradigm—supported at its foundation by the "creative" to the "ideal" conscience—which is at the heart of all this Faith deterioration. Also, it is the source of energy and commitment for Collective Split-Conscience™, a collaborative pathway disconnected from Salvation which is also known as "groupthink".

✝ *Jesus answered, "Amen, amen, I say to you, no one can enter the kingdom of God without being born of water and Spirit."*
—John 3:5
The New American Bible 1987

Following the spiritual Born Again experience of Saint Nicodemus—directly speaking with Jesus Christ as he was schooled—the Church around the world needs to stop presenting a false Salvation Pathway by advocating that pastors, preachers, and others in religious leadership, replace the Holy Spirit in the human conscience. This is misleading and deceiving to millions of the Faithful who seek the truth of Jesus Christ for Salvation.

At the Last Supper, Jesus told the Apostles the Holy Spirit would come after him...

✝ *And I will ask the Father, and He will give you another Advocate to be with you always, the Spirit of truth...*
—John 14:16-17
The New American Bible 1987

—— III ——

DEFEATING HERESY AND APOSTASY

• DENIAL OF TRUTH (HERESY)
• FAILURE IN FAITH | SCANDAL TO OTHER CHRISTIANS (APOSTASY)

Heresy—"the obstinate denial or doubt, on the part of a baptized person, of a truth that must be believed by divine and Catholic faith. The First Vatican Council... declared that by divine and catholic faith all those things must be believed that are contained in the word of God, whether written or handed down, and have been proposed by the Church, whether by solemn judgment or by its ordinary universal magisterium, as divinely revealed..."

—Encyclopedia of Catholicism
HarperCollins Publishers, Inc., 1995, 610-611

Apostasy—"the complete and public rejection of the faith into which one has been baptized and of all the Church's teaching. Apostasy is distinguished from heresy, by which one rejects a part of the Church's teaching while still claiming membership in the Church. According to Roman Catholic canon law, an unrepentant apostate is excluded from the sacraments."

—Encyclopedia of Catholicism
HarperCollins Publishers, Inc.,1995, 73

23

Heresy and Apostasy are embedded in and help empower the gravely Immoral Slippery Slope which began with Radical Feminism's "No Room in the Womb" for a child of God. This anti-God's Plan of Generations human construct— configured decades ago "out of thin air" by the U.S. Supreme Court— jump started the wide-spread and rapidly growing Immoral Slippery Slope:

"Go Along to Get Along" Personal Paradigm & Lifestyle, Over Time, Results In...

Immoral Slippery Slope
Includes Recent Downward Acceleration

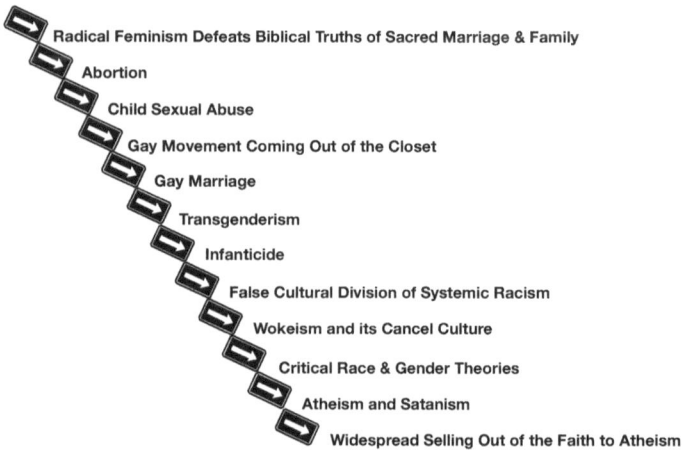

→ Radical Feminism Defeats Biblical Truths of Sacred Marriage & Family
→ Abortion
→ Child Sexual Abuse
→ Gay Movement Coming Out of the Closet
→ Gay Marriage
→ Transgenderism
→ Infanticide
→ False Cultural Division of Systemic Racism
→ Wokeism and its Cancel Culture
→ Critical Race & Gender Theories
→ Atheism and Satanism
→ Widespread Selling Out of the Faith to Atheism

DENIAL OF TRUTH
LEADS TO FAILURE IN FAITH

While the Immoral Slippery Slope continues to slide downward rapidly, *Amoris Laetitia* is unfortunately the Vatican's current conscience teachings that replace the Holy Spirit with the pastor:
"...discernment is dynamic:..."
"...ever open to new stages of growth..."
"...new decisions which can enable the ideal to be more fully realized..."
—*Amoris Laetitia*, Apostolic Exhortation (2016)
Chapter 8, Pgs. 233-235, Para.302/303

24

Amoris Laetitia is in direct conflict with the infallible and earlier moral teachings of Saint Pope John Paul II's *Veritatis Splendor* — The Splendor of Truth—as he clearly explains:

> ✝ *... an attempt is made to legitimize so called 'pastoral' solutions contrary to the teaching of the Magisterium, and justify a 'creative' hermeneutic according to which the moral conscience is in no way obligated, in every case, by a particular negative precept.*
>
> *No one can fail to realize that these approaches pose a challenge to the very identity of the moral conscience in relation to human freedom and God's law.*
>
> —Saint Pope John Paul II
> *Veritatis Splendor*, Pauline Books & Media, 74-75

"CREATIVE" IS FOR BRANDING, POSITIONING & MARKETING—NOT CONSCIENCES

A "creative" conscience facilitates and encourages the separation of freedom and truth while having high appeal to "self-styled" Catholics that rely upon "situation ethics" and a "Go Along to Get Along" personal paradigm.

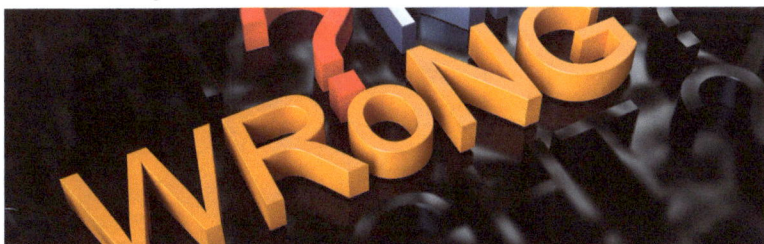

This ignoring of God allows unfaithful messages to be fully considered in the human mind that originate in the heart. Therefore, "creative to ideal" conscience disrupts the heart and the mind with unholy work that also generates personal stress as the mind becomes focused on fleshly-centric thinking and related processes.

Saint Pope John Paul II further counsels about judgment of conscience:

The maturity and responsibility of these judgments— and, when all is said and done, of the individual who is their subject—are not measured by the liberation of the conscience from objective truth, in favor of an alleged autonomy in personal decisions, but, on the contrary, by an insistent search for truth and by allowing oneself to be guided by that truth in one's actions.

—Saint Pope John Paul II
Veritatis Splendor, Pauline Books & Media, 78-79

FAILURE IN FAITH
SCANDAL TO ALL CHRISTIANS

It appears that the significant success of the Immoral Slippery Slope has influenced the leadership of the Catholic Church to essentially teach that one can be simultaneously "in" and "out" as a Catholic while easing the pain of related grave sin by helping evolve the person's conscience from the "creative" to the "ideal" so it will fit for the "self-styled". Apparently, this is the current leadership of the Catholic Church's way of "living with" the Immoral Slippery Slope which is chock full of gravely immoral sins that feed heresy and apostasy and which oppose God's Plan of Generations.

CONSCIENCE WARRIORS GO INTO THE HEAT OF THE TRUTH BATTLE WHEN FAITH IS ON THE LINE

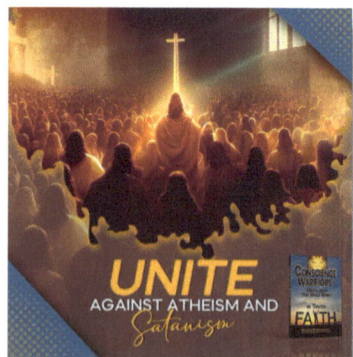

UNITE
AGAINST ATHEISM AND *Satanism*

Saint Joseph of Arimathea—the first Conscience Warrior— went into the heat of the truth battle and broke away from the fleshly grip of the Pharisees' and the Sanhedrin's Collective Split-Conscience™ and its "group think".

Following in Joseph's Faithful leadership and footsteps, today's Conscience Warriors Unite with the Holy Spirit in Truth in the personal conscience and fight endlessly to protect, promote, champion, and win for God's Plan of Generations.

Why is this a battle? God's Plan of Generations is currently being torn apart in homes, schools, doctor's offices, hospitals, clinics, and churches, by parents, teachers, doctors, psychologists, counselors, priests, pastors, and many others whose consciences are not United with the Holy Spirit in Truth.

✝ *Now the Spirit manifestly saith that in the last times some shall depart from the faith, giving heed to spirits of error and doctrines of devils. Speaking lies in hypocrisy and having their conscience seared.*
— 1 Timothy 4:1-2
The Douay Bible 1941

CONSCIENCE WARRIORS WILL ALWAYS FIGHT TO SAVE THE INNOCENT

We will go into battle every moment to defeat gaslighting and virtue signaling which are the destructive psychological techniques that rely on Collective Split-Conscience and that trade-off and override Faithful personal conscience.

We will expose these techniques that are also part of effective modern day communications tools of the powerful to help cover-up lies and promote nefarious agendas. Agendas like teaching children and young adults that God made them the wrong gender, God makes mistakes, and that they can make themselves better than God could ever have imagined in His wildest dreams! This nefarious and evil agenda teaches Atheism and Satanism to children and young adults and is immoral to the core.

✠ *Whoever is not with me is against me, and whoever does not gather with me scatters. Therefore, I say to you, every sin and blasphemy will be forgiven people, but blasphemy against the Spirit will not be forgiven. And whoever speaks a word against the Son of Man will be forgiven; but whoever speaks against the Holy Spirit will not be forgiven, either in this age or in the age to come.*
—Matthew 12:30-32
The New American Bible 1987

At the Last Supper, Jesus told the Apostles the Holy Spirit would come after him...

✠ *The Advocate, the Holy Spirit that the Father will send in my name—he will teach you everything and remind you of all that [I] told you.*
—John 14:26
The New American Bible 1987

Conscience Warriors go into the heat of the truth battle when today's culture puts their Faith on the line. Personal conscience needs to be addressed, embraced openly and honestly.

Christ's prayer for his disciples...

✠ *Consecrate them in the truth. Your word is truth. As you sent me into the world, so I sent them into the world. And I consecrate myself to them, so that they also many be consecrated in truth.*
—John 17:17-19
The New American Bible 1987

The Holy Spirit is always available to light up the Faithful for navigating a successful pathway through the narrow gate.
The Holy Spirit
Divine Counselor • Spirit of Truth
Spirit of Love • Spirit of Peace

—— IV ——

DYSFUNCTIONAL CONSCIENCES OF THE WOKE WORLD— BREAK FREE FROM THE CHAINS OF EVIL SOCIETAL CONFORMITY

Children and young adults are being taught and groomed in many American schools—public, private, Christian, and Catholic schools—to be Atheists and Satanists when they are fed numerous and ongoing lies about their gender, race, pronouns, and all the "mistakes" that God makes. They are being taught that God is fallible or doesn't exist; and that possibly Satan is their real savior.

Critical race and gender theories, wokeism, cancel culture, gender dysphoria, transgenderism, and all related teachings must be defeated. These gravely immoral and evil actions— if aligned with, agreed to, and championed—can destroy the practice of Christianity, along with the nuclear family and God's Plan of Generations.

The Holy Bible's Sacred Scripture is essentially being thrown into the fire and burned even by some religious and political leaders, parents, doctors, counselors, school officials, corporations, and lawmakers, just to name a few.

Now—on college campuses—vending machines are being installed to dispense chemical abortion pills that not only kill a child of God; these pills may also do grave harm to those who consume them.

Are you being overwhelmed by people in your life advocating evil practices, laws, policies, and procedures surrounding your every move?

Are you being fed a false and evil paradigm to just let it all happen, "Go Along to Get Along", and not dare to disagree, ask questions, or speak the truth?

Are you upset when American flags are being tossed aside or torn down to make room for whatever the money changers flaunt for more money, power, and glory?

When are we going to shake off the Culture of Death's clever brainwash that splits, sears, and brands consciences making them dysfunctional? When are we gong to thoroughly and comprehensively understand that the counsel and strength provided by the Holy Spirit in our conscience leads the way to a Faithful and integrated heart and mind which generates the intellectual integrity needed for Salvation?

EMBARK ON A QUEST TO EXPOSE THE LIES

Let us all take a stand against the Immoral Slippery Slope and help restore the true moral compass of our society. None of us should be nonchalant about gaining a biblically based understanding of personal conscience.

We must all Unite with the Holy Spirit in Truth to ensure that we thoroughly understand and follow the Salvation pathway. It is available to all of us as provided by Jesus Christ on Pentecost. Let us stand firm in our Faith. Let us all be witnesses to the power of personal repentance, conversion, and redemption by taking the lead necessary for personal Salvation. Empower your conscience. Help save lives and souls. Defend and champion Faith and Truth.

GO INTO THE HEAT OF THE TRUTH BATTLE WHEN FAITH IS ON THE LINE

As Conscience Warriors, you can become a unyielding force to help extricate and save families from present day evil. Conscience Warriors will prayerfully and peacefully win the spiritual battle for Catholicism, Christianity, Judeo-Christian principles, and God's Plan of Generations.

> *Amen I say to you, if you have faith and do not waiver, not only will you do what has been done to the fig tree, but even if you say to this mountain, 'Be lifted up and thrown into the sea,' it will be done. "Whatsoever you shall ask for in prayer, with faith, you will receive."*
> —Matthew 21:21-22
> The New American Bible, 1987

FAITHFUL GUARDIANS *Truth*

God's Plan of Generations

—— V ——

SAINT POPE TO WOKE POPE— SACRED SCRIPTURE VS. SYNOD'S METHODOLOGY

With your help we can win the Spiritual conscience battle. Let's examine the critical preaching polarity between two modern day Popes.

How can God's people be on and dedicated to a Salvation pathway when the human conscience is not faithfully understood as preached in the Bible?

> *I charge you in the presence of God and of Christ Jesus, who will judge the living and the dead, and by his appearing and his kingly power: proclaim the word; be persistent whether it is convenient or inconvenient; convince, reprimand, encourage through all patience and teaching. For the time will come when people will not tolerate sound doctrine but, following their own desires and insatiable curiosity, will accumulate teachers and will stop listening to the truth and will be diverted to myths.*
> — 2 Timothy 4:1-4
> The New American Bible 1987

✝

...may you fight a good fight by having faith and a good
conscience. Some, by rejecting conscience,
have made a shipwreck of their faith.
— 1 Timothy 1:18-19
The New American Bible 1987

To the clean all things are clean, but to those who are
defiled and unbelieving nothing is clean; in fact,
both their minds and their consciences are tainted.
— Titus 1:15
The New American Bible 1987

What makes the human conscience misunderstood today? Unfortunately, it's about the critical preaching polarity between two modern day Popes — Saint Pope John Paul II and Pope Francis.

SAINT POPE JOHN PAUL II

Saint Pope John Paul II (JPII) lays out the fundamental truths about conscience in his Encyclical *Dominum et Vivificantem* (The Holy Spirit in The Life of The Church and The World), May 18, 1986, the 8th year of his Pontificate. He addresses the challenges of the heretical thought process of solely the human mind in one's conscience.

The action of the Spirit of truth, which works toward the
salvific "convincing concerning sin," encounters in a
person in this condition an interior resistance, as it were
an impenetrability of conscience, a state of mind which
could be described as fixed by reason of a free choice.
This is what Sacred Scripture usually calls "hardness of
heart." In our own time this attitude of mind and heart is
perhaps reflected in the loss of the sense of sin,...
— Saint Pope John Paul II
Dominum et Vivificantem
Pauline Books & Media 1986, 79-80

✝ *...people fall back on their personal conscience but forget that this conscience is the eye that does not of itself possess light, but only when it looks to the authentic source of light.*
— Saint Pope John Paul II
Agenda For The Third Millennium, World Chapter, 172

JPII continues with the pathway to Salvation in *Dominum et Vivificantem:*

✝ *Those who let themselves be "convinced concerning sin" by the Holy Spirit, also allow themselves to be convinced "concerning righteousness and judgment." In this righteousness the Holy Spirit, the Spirit of the Father and the Son, who "convinces the world concerning sin," reveals himself and makes himself present in man as the Spirit of eternal life.*
— Saint Pope John Paul II
Dominum et Vivificantem
Pauline Books & Media 1986, 81-82

POPE FRANCIS

Pope Francis is obviously more interested in directing fellow Catholics that his or her pastor can replace the Holy Spirit in the personal conscience by a human method of confident choosing—while building a personal "creative to the ideal" conscience over time—irrespective of ignoring/violating God's commandments.

His 2016 (post 2014 & 2015 Synods) Apostolic Exhortation *Amoris Laetitia* (The Joy of Love) states the following in Chapter 8, paragraph 303, pages 234-235.

"Yet conscience can do more than recognize that a given situation does not correspond objectively to the overall demands of the Gospel. It can also recognize with sincerity and honesty what for now is the most generous response which can be given to God, and come to see with a certain moral security that it is what God himself is asking amid the concrete complexity of one's limits, while yet not fully the objective ideal. And...In any event, let us recall that this discernment is dynamic; it must remain ever open to new stages of growth and to new decisions which can enable the ideal to be more full realized."*

*Underlining by Author.

The above certainly makes clear that the person leads God in the conscience which we know is heretical to our beloved Faith!

WHO IS YOUR CONSCIENCE FOLLOWING?
SAINT POPE JOHN PAUL II
OR
WOKE POPE FRANCIS?

Pope Francis' preaching and teaching that the human conscience is guided and counseled by the pastor to a "creative to ideal" development that empowers "situation ethics" driven by personal choice without the Holy Spirit is obviously NOT part of the Salvation Pathway that Jesus Christ preached.

The Salvation Pathway requires confession, repentance, and conversion to avoid heresy and the horrors of apostasy.

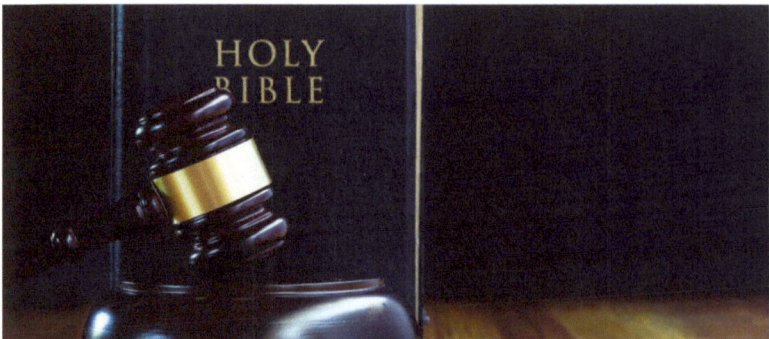

—— VI ——

SACRED SCRIPTURE VS.
SYNOD ON SYNODALITY

The Church in Synod on Synodality: "A New Way of Being"? Does the Pope believe in the Holy Bible?

Pope Francis explains in *Amoris Laetitia*, Chapter 8, Para.303, pp. 234-235 the "ideal" conscience: "...discernment is dynamic; it must remain ever open to new stages of growth and to new decisions which can enable the ideal to be more fully realized."

Without the existence of *Amoris Laetitia*, the current Synod would be without proper authority to proceed; further, *Amoris Laetitia* requires personal consciences that have been silenced with God replaced!

Yes, the above quote from *Amoris Laetitia* requires a Godless personal conscience! This Godless requirement for the "creative to the ideal"[1] empowering a "situation ethics"[1] conscience assists a "Go Along to Get Along" personal paradigm which forecloses the Holy Spirit and evaporates over time the intellectual integrity needed in order to remain on a Salvation Pathway.[1]

INTELLECTUAL INTEGRITY EVAPORATES

A "creative to the ideal" conscience evaporates intellectual integrity by living "according to the flesh" which demands flexibility of conscience to convince oneself that human logic alone must prevail with decision making. In other words, the person is unable to sustain intellectual integrity which is evaporated by the heat of an emotionally-centric manipulation of the Faithful synthesis of conscience, heart, and mind as he/she morphs into a "self-styled" Catholic/Christian further empowering "situation ethics".[1]

TRUTH, PURITY, INTEGRITY

Jesus demonstrates and teaches us that Truth in the Conscience, Purity of Heart, and the Mind's Intellectual Integrity expose embedded lies and gaslighting attempts. For those lies and gaslighting attempts occurring in the 2023 Synod on Synodality are exploitation tools of the devil—in the deeply nefarious pathway of personal gain and protection from loss—to empty out souls by the human embrace and practice of Satanism.

"If you are the Son of God, command this stone to become bread." Jesus answered him, "It is written, 'One does not live by bread alone.'"
—Luke 4:3-4
The New American Bible 1987

Jesus understands the devil's evil attempts embedded with lies and connected to the corrupt, satanic promises of money, power, and glory:

✝ *Then he took him up and showed him all the kingdoms of the world in a single instant. The devil said to him: "I shall give to you all this power and their glory; for it has been handed over to me, and I may give it to whomever I wish. All this will be yours, if you worship me." Jesus said to him in reply, "It is written: You shall worship the Lord, your God, and him alone shall you serve".*
—Luke 4:5-8
The New American Bible 1987

The devil's gaslighting continues:

✝ *Then he led him to Jerusalem, made him stand on the parapet of the temple, and said to him. "If you are the Son of God, throw yourself down from here, for it is written: 'He will command his angels concerning you to guard you', and 'With their hands they will support you, 'lest you dash your foot against a stone.'" Jesus said to him in reply, "It also says, 'You shall not put the Lord, your God, to the test.'"*
—Luke 4:9-13
The New American Bible 1987

SYNOD ON SYNODALITY'S METHODOLOGY DEFINES A "NEW WAY OF BEING" PERSONAL CONSCIENCE

Pope Francis' preaching and teaching that the human conscience is guided and counseled by the pastor to a "creative to ideal"[1] development that empowers "situation ethics"[1] driven by personal choice without the Holy Spirit is clearly NOT part of the Salvation Pathway that Jesus Christ preached.

The 2023 Synod needs to condemn—not promote—what is currently going on in the Immoral Slippery Slope which is getting worse every moment of every day.

"Go Along to Get Along" Personal Paradigm & Lifestyle, Over Time, Results In...

Immoral Slippery Slope

Includes Recent Downward Acceleration

Radical Feminism Defeats Biblical Truths of Sacred Marriage & Family

Abortion

Child Sexual Abuse

Gay Movement Coming Out of the Closet

Gay Marriage

Transgenderism

Infanticide

False Cultural Division of Systemic Racism

Wokeism and its Cancel Culture

Critical Race & Gender Theories

Atheism and Satanism

Widespread Selling Out of the Faith to Atheism

Here is Saint Pope John Paul II's 1993 warning of the potential danger zone ahead if the pastoral is elevated and the Holy Spirit is eliminated in the personal conscience:

...an attempt is made to legitimize so called "pastoral" solutions contrary to the teaching of the Magisterium, and justify a 'creative' hermeneutic according to which the moral conscience is in no way obligated, in every case, by a particular negative precept.

✝ *No one can fail to realize that these approaches pose a challenge to the very identity of the moral conscience in relation to human freedom and God's law.*

—Saint Pope John Paul II
Veritatis Splendor
Pauline Books & Media, 74-75

1. Archbishop Carlo Maria Viganò, Former Apostolic Nuncio to the United States, recent writings.

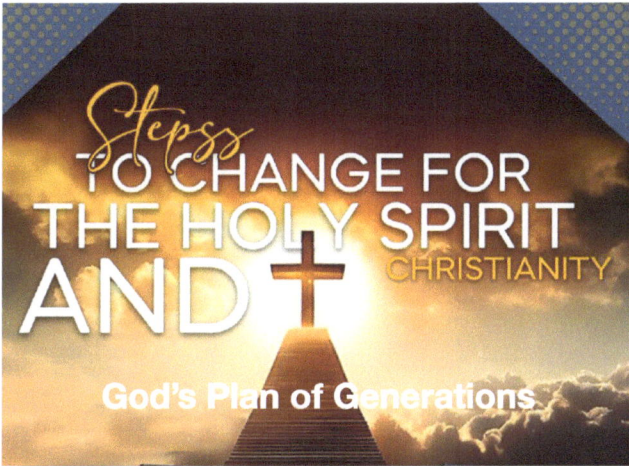

A Prayer for the Intercession of

Saint Jerome — Truth
Saint Anthony the Great — Purity of Heart
Saint Augustine of Hippo — Intellectual Integrity

Pray for us in our deep and arduous struggle
to respond to a major heresy of our time
—Radical Feminism—
the beginning of the Immoral Slippery Slope.

Pray for us as we advocate for the
union of Freedom and Truth
to Faithfully help protect the root of fruitfulness
in Sacred Marriage and Family.

In your names, we fervently pray
for your Intercession for a return to the truth
of the full embrace of God's Plan of Generations.

Amen

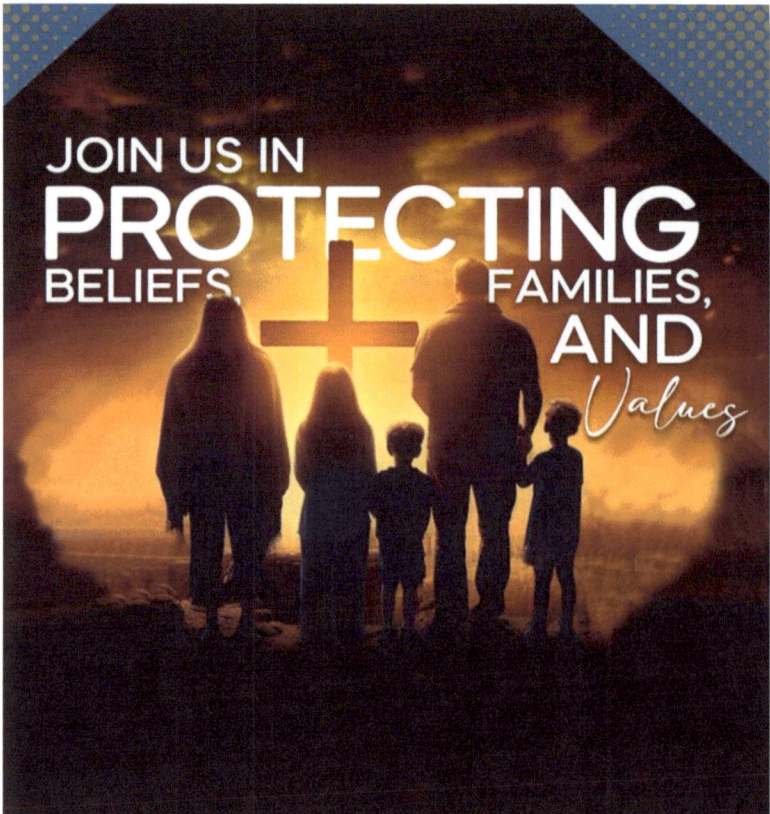

JOIN US IN PROTECTING BELIEFS, FAMILIES, AND *Values*

—— VII ——

WOKE POPE SUBSTITUTES BLESSING FOR REPENTANCE & CONVERSION

Anyone paying attention to the leadership of the Catholic Church today would be readily aware of the makings of a deep moral division recently accelerated with the Woke Pope's substitution of Blessing for Repentance & Conversion. The issue originates with the obliteration of God-given sexuality differences and God's Plan of Generations.

As Saint Pope John Paul II has written:

> *If Jesus says that blasphemy against the Holy Spirit cannot be forgiven either in this life or in the next, it is because this "non forgiveness" is linked, as to its cause, to "non-repentance," in other words to the radical refusal to be converted.*

> *Blasphemy against the Holy Spirit, then, is the sin committed by the person who claims to have a "right" to persist in evil—in any sin at all— and who thus rejects Redemption.*
> —Saint Pope John Paul II
> *Dominum et Vivificantem,*
> Pauline Books & Media 1986, 79

SUPPORTIVE CATHOLICS OF THE WOKE POPE CONVOLUTE TRUTH

Those aligned with the Pope's homosexual messages that bear on confusion in explanation and promotion, defend him vigorously along the argumentative lines that the Woke Pope is not blessing—in any way whatsoever—same sex unions; however, simply put, these so-called Woke Pope supportive Catholics convolute truth when vigorously explaining/declaring that the Pope is only blessing the individuals and not the unions of same sex Catholics.

> ✝ *If you believe what you like in the gospels, and reject what you don't like, it is not the gospel you believe, but yourself.*
> —St. Augustine of Hippo
> The Confessions of St. Augustine

OUR WOKE POPE CONVOLUTES THE TRUTH WITH A CONFUSING/NON-BIBLICAL "WORK AROUND"

Considering the consistently documented truth of Sacred Scripture over thousands of years and the authority of the Catholic Magisterium, how is this twisting of truth possible? Obviously, common sense tells us that this sort of attempted "work around" of Sacred Scripture and the Catholic Magisterium doesn't fly given its hot link to "non-repentance" for two individuals choosing a same sex union that—to begin with— is the fundamental motivator for the Pope's "personal blessings".

Obviously, our Woke Pope is clearly ignoring his complete and profound knowledge of the difference between sacred Communio that lovingly and always pre-supposes God[1]— as our Creator and includes the Pascal Mystery, Jesus' Hypostatic Union and His Consubstantial Act of sending the

Holy Spirit to all mankind on Pentecost—with all human activity.

✝ *"The Church...instructed by the words of Christ, and drawing on the experience of Pentecost and her own apostolic history, has proclaimed since the earliest centuries her faith in the Holy Spirit, as 'the giver of life', the one 'in whom' the inscrutable 'Triune God communicates himself to human beings', constituting in them the source of eternal life."*
—Saint Pope John Paul II
Dominum et Vivificantem
Pauline Books & Media 1986, 8

A DIRECT ATTACK ON GOD'S PLAN OF GENERATIONS

Why ignore the truth of God's Plan of Generations that our Woke Pope has known and embraced for many decades? Why does the Woke Pope continue to pursue word salads—that evaporate intellectual integrity—to convince and capture Catholics and all Christians with and/or developing split-consciences, branded/seared consciences, and collective consciences to push aside Repentance & Conversion which are an integral part of the Salvation Pathway?

In his Agenda for the Third Millennium, 1996, Saint Pope John Paul II offers a fundamental starting point for understanding and avoiding Split, Branded/Seared, and/or Collective Conscience:

✝ *...people fall back on their personal conscience but forget that this conscience is the eye that does not of itself possess light, but only when it looks to the authentic source of light.*
— Saint Pope John Paul II
Agenda For The Third Millennium, World Chapter, 172

45

Saint Pope John Paul II addresses the challenges of the heretical thought process of solely the human mind in one's conscience:

> *The action of the Spirit of truth, which works toward the salvific "convincing concerning sin," encounters in a person in this condition an interior resistance, as it were an impenetrability of conscience, a state of mind which could be described as fixed by reason of a free choice. This is what Sacred Scripture usually calls "hardness of heart." In our own time this attitude of mind and heart is perhaps reflected in the loss of the sense of sin,...*
> — Saint Pope John Paul II
> *Dominum et Vivificantem*,
> Pauline Books & Media 1986, 79-80

To intellectually engage, prop up, champion, and enthusiastically promote a "Go Along to Get Along" sexual relations construct and paradigm does not presuppose God with all human activity. It is and will continue to be a direct attack against the Sacred Scripture teachings about God's Plan of Generations.

Saint Pope John Paul II continues with the pathway to Salvation:

> *Those who let themselves be "convinced concerning sin" by the Holy Spirit, also allow themselves to be convinced "concerning righteousness and judgment." In this righteousness the Holy Spirit, the Spirit of the Father and the Son, who "convinces the world concerning sin," reveals himself and makes himself present in man as the Spirit of eternal life.*
> — Saint Pope John Paul II
> *Dominum et Vivificantem*,
> Pauline Books & Media 1986, 81-82

AMORIS LAETITIA'S HUMAN ONLY
PASTORAL CONSCIENCE

Saint Pope John Paul II explains this current sexual heresy—intellectually justified by Pope Francis' Roman Catholic Apostolic Exhortation (2016) *Amoris Laetitia's* heretical Chapter 8, 303: pages 234-235 concerning a new, human idea that a "creative to the ideal" conscience is in reference to the evolving of the "objective ideal" (which is outside "… the overall demands of the Gospel.")—is utterly devoid of the repentance promptings of the Holy Spirit in the human conscience as it replaces the Holy Spirit with the pastor in the human conscience.

> *The Holy Spirit, then, will ensure that in the Church there will always continue 'the same truth' which the Apostles heard from their Master.*
> —Saint Pope John Paul II
> *Dominum et Vivificantem*
> Pauline Books & Media 1986, 14

Pope Benedict XVI certainly affirms his predecessor:
> *"We wish to make clear that departure from the Church's teaching, or silence about it, in an effort to provide pastoral care is neither caring nor pastoral."*
> —Cardinal Joseph Ratzinger, Pope Benedict XVI

Jesus issues stern warnings to his disciples:
> *"Whoever is not with me is against me, and whoever does not gather with me scatters. Therefore, I say to you, every sin and blasphemy will be forgiven people, but blasphemy against the Spirit will not be forgiven. And whoever speaks a word against the Son of Man will be forgiven, but whoever speaks against the Holy Spirit will not be forgiven, either in this age or in the age to come."*
> —Matthew 12:30-32
> The New American Bible 1987

As Conscience Warriors aligned with our Almighty God, we must all rise up, join together, and embrace the power of the living example of Jesus Christ—while being guided to Salvation by our Counselor, the Holy Spirit—and peacefully protect our faith, our families, and our precious, innocent children from all these grave evils.

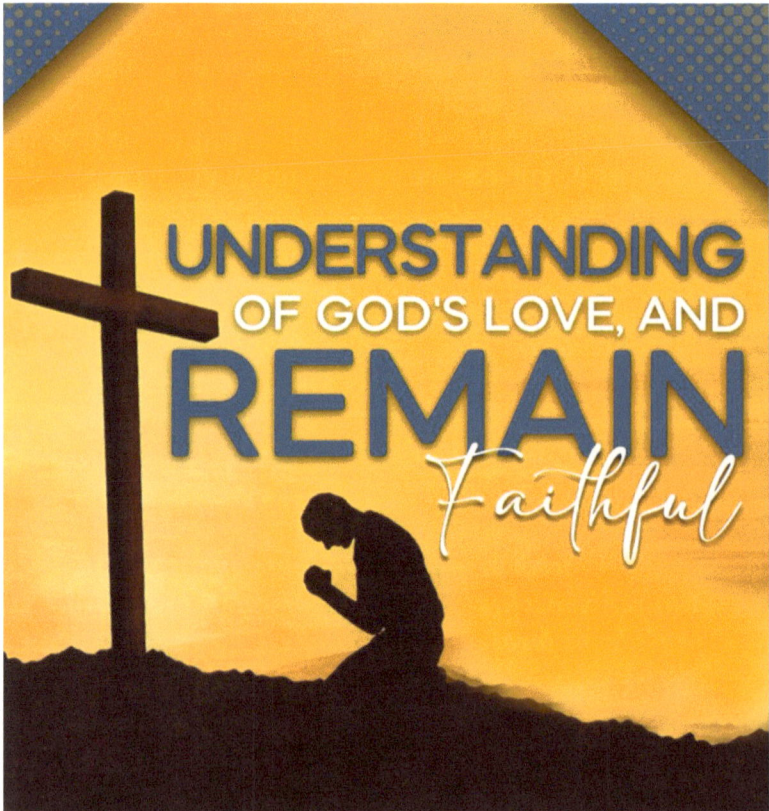

But you, man of God, avoid all this. Instead, pursue righteousness, devotion, faith, love, patience, and gentleness. Compete well for the faith. Lay hold of eternal life...
—1 Timothy 6:11-12
The New American Bible 1987

LISTEN TO THE HOLY SPIRIT

"The Church...instructed by the words of Christ, and drawing on the experience of Pentecost and her own apostolic history, has proclaimed since the earliest centuries her faith in the Holy Spirit, as 'the giver of life', the one 'in whom' the inscrutable 'Triune God communicates himself to human beings', constituting in them the source of eternal life."
—Saint Pope John Paul II
Dominum et Vivificantem,
Pauline Books & Media 1986, 8

✝

"...an attempt is made to legitimize so called "pastoral" solutions contrary to the teaching of the Magisterium, and justify a 'creative' hermeneutic according to which the moral conscience is in no way obligated, in every case, by a particular negative precept. No one can fail to realize that these approaches pose a challenge to the 'very identity of the moral conscience' in relation to human freedom and God's law."
—Saint Pope John Paul II
Veritatis Splendor
Pauline Books & Media, 74-75

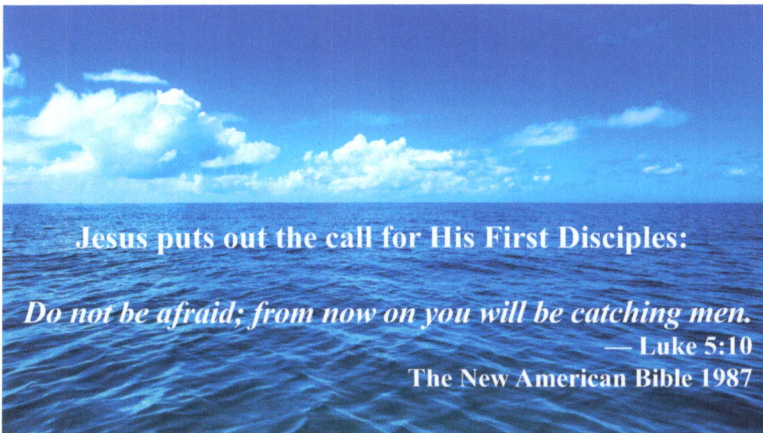

Jesus puts out the call for His First Disciples:

Do not be afraid; from now on you will be catching men.
— Luke 5:10
The New American Bible 1987

1. David L. Schindler, *Ordering Love*, 2011

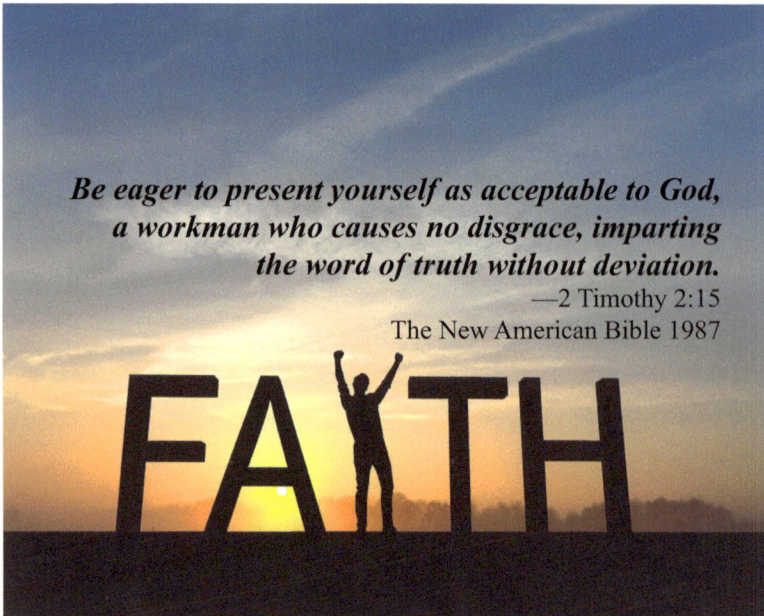

Be eager to present yourself as acceptable to God, a workman who causes no disgrace, imparting the word of truth without deviation.
—2 Timothy 2:15
The New American Bible 1987

—— VIII ——

DISPLACED FEAR FUELS
THAT MAN IS GOD

THESE TWO MEN SPIRITUALLY AND BRAVELY
BROKE AWAY FROM COLLECTIVE SPLIT-CONSCIENCE

Joseph of Arimathea and Nicodemus—both wealthy and members of the high society of their times—started their "breakout journeys" by pressing towards Jesus Christ, the Son of God. They broke away from the dangerous Collective Split-Conscience of their times (formed and carried out with the human techniques of Group Think, Brain Wash, and the misplaced fear of man) and worked on building their relationships directly with Jesus. They both knew, in their own way, that loving and fearing God were essential concerning their pathways to Salvation.

Today, we are surrounded by Catholics and many other Christians that are assisting the further fueling of the Immoral Slippery Slope to the point of completely displacing God by energizing and promoting that man himself is God. How much of this would be reality today without a Woke Pope and a plethora of "self-styled" and "devout" Catholics with substantial power carrying out "situation ethics"? How much of this evil leadership, fueled with satanic behavior, would be active and growing today without the "license" to artificially displace the Holy Spirit in the human moral conscience?

As Saint Pope John Paul II has written:

> *Those who reject the fundamental truth of things, who set themselves up as the yardstick of everything, and thus put themselves in God's place; who more or less consciously think they can do without God, the Creator of the world, or without Christ, the Redeemer of the human race; who instead of seeking God run back to idols, will always turn their backs on the one supreme and fundamental truth.*
> —Saint Pope John Paul II
> *Agenda for The Third Millennium*, Faith Chapter, 9
> Homily for Young People, Munich, 19 November 1980

Amoris Laetitia —
THE OFFICIAL CURRENT DAY EVIL "LICENSE"

This current day evil "license"— the "legitimate" beginning of the Group Think that fuels a Go Along to Get Along paradigm and supports Collective Split-Conscience™— commissioned in Catholic dictum by the Woke Pope's heretical *Amoris Laetitia* (2016) labeled as a Roman Catholic Apostolic Exhortation. Chapter 8, pages 233-235, and directly in paragraphs 302 & 303, layout the "creative to the ideal" conscience which is the official birthplace of the Collective Conscience on an epidemic scale published by the Woke Pope. The official Catholic "license" to accept, empower, and promote evil on a scale never seen before in the world that we live in.

Amazingly, the Immoral Slippery Slope which began with Radical Feminism has "advanced"—further downward— to an accelerated, persistent, and dangerous assault on the innocence of our children to the point of using what the Woke world deceptively labels as "gender dysphoria" as too much for parents to handle. Therefore, parents are now obsolete and incapable of handling what is nothing more than raising their children as believing and practicing Christians. Further, as an assault on Christianity itself, many Catholic Churches will soon be having "pride masses" conducted throughout America! All of this represents a major and dangerous negative impact on Marriage & Family and God's Plan of Generations.

BREAKING THE LINK BETWEEN FREEDOM AND TRUTH

Here are the evil yet "successful" human building blocks along the way in time that heretically brake the link between freedom and truth:

1. Split-Conscience™
2. Go Along to Get Along Personal Behavior
3. Branded/Seared Conscience
4. "Creative to the Ideal" Conscience
   "licensed" by the Woke Pope (2016)
5. Collective Split-Conscience™

Saint Pope John Paul II writes:

The way in which one conceives the relationship between freedom and law is thus intimately bound up with one's understanding of the moral conscience. Here the cultural tendencies referred to above — in which freedom and law are set in opposition to each other and kept apart, and freedom is exalted almost to the point of idolatry — lead to a "creative" understanding of moral conscience, which diverges from the teaching of the Church's tradition and her Magisterium.
—Saint Pope John Paul II
Veritatis Splendor, Pauline Books & Media, 73

HUMAN ONLY PASTORAL CONSCIENCE

Saint Pope John Paul II further explains this current heresy of conscience—intellectually justified and "licensed" by *Amoris Laetitia's* heretical Chapter 8, pages 233-235, and directly in paragraphs 302 & 303, concerning a new, human idea that a "creative to the ideal" conscience is in reference to the evolving of the "objective ideal" (which is outside "… the overall demands of the Gospel.")—is utterly devoid of the repentance promptings of the Holy Spirit in the human conscience as it displaces the Holy Spirit with the pastor in the human conscience.

> *...an attempt is made to legitimize so called "pastoral" solutions contrary to the teaching of the Magisterium, and justify a 'creative' hermeneutic according to which the moral conscience is in no way obligated, in every case, by a particular negative precept. No one can fail to realize that these approaches pose a challenge to the 'very identity of the moral conscience' in relation to human freedom and God's law.*
> —Saint Pope John Paul II
> *Veritatis Splendor*
> Pauline Books & Media, 74-75

✝

> *The "guiding into all the truth" is therefore achieved in faith and through faith: and this is the work of the Spirit of truth and the result of his action in man.*
> —Saint Pope John Paul II
> *Dominum et Vivificantem*
> Pauline Books & Media 1986, 15

Pope Benedict XVI affirms his predecessor:

> *We wish to make clear that departure from the Church's teaching, or silence about it, in an effort to provide pastoral care is neither caring nor pastoral.*
> —Cardinal Joseph Ratzinger, Pope Benedict XVI

—— IX ——

THE WORLD IS ON FIRE—
A REVOLUTION OF CONSCIENCE
IS NEEDED NOW

The world is on fire. A religious fire. Yet, what everyone in the world still has in common is a personal conscience. On Pentecost, Jesus sent the Holy Spirit to be with all of us in our consciences as our Salvation Counselor.

Similar to the late twentieth century Cold War era, our world currently has a massive conscience malfunction. In the eighties, Saint Pope John Paul II and our great President Ronald Reagan worked together and essentially bankrupted the USSR which defeated its communism regime. Saint Pope John Paul II focused on creating a Revolution of Conscience and President Reagan focused on defeating the USSR's economy. This high-level team effort was very successful for the benefit of the entire world.

A GREAT FOREST PLANTED BY
AROUSED CONSCIENCES

George Weigel has written volumes about Saint Pope John Paul II—as his official biographer—and recently declared

"The west needs its own version of JPII's 'Revolution of Conscience'. Weigel shared that a friend of John Paul II, a philosopher-priest named Joseph Tishner, had once described the anti-communist movement inspired Pope, as "a great forest planted by aroused consciences."

"Father Tischner's brilliant image is one that bears reflection today," Weigel wrote, concluding: "For the West needs 'reforestation' a planting of new seeds of conscience, reflecting the built-in truths about human dignity to which John Paul II appealed during those nine days of June 1979."

Unfortunately, we do not have Saint Pope John Paul's help in the flesh today with our challenges of socialism, marxism, communism, and its related atheism and satanism. However, we have the Gospel and the soul-saving moral lessons directly from Jesus Christ Himself to Saint Nicodemus that bear on the most important of all:

> *Now there was a Pharisee named Nicodemus, a ruler of the Jews. He came to Jesus at night and said to him, "Rabbi, we know that you are a teacher who has come from God, for no one can do these signs that you are doing unless God is with him." Jesus answered and said to him, "Amen, amen, I say to you, no one can see the kingdom of God without being born from above."*
> —John 3:1-3
> The New American Bible 1987

We know that Nicodemus was a Pharisee and an influential member of the ruling council, the Sanhedrin. His interactions with Jesus in John 3:1-21, are foundational theological teaching on being "born again", "born of the Spirit."

SPIRITUAL REBIRTH AND TRANSFORMATION

A Spiritual Rebirth and Transformation—foundational and central to Christian Faith and Salvation today—clearly requires immediate alienation from the Immoral Slippery Slope which is growing rapidly and now includes gender dysphoria promotion.

The United States of America has entered into a state of extreme Nuclear Family dismemberment that is tearing down the heart of God's Plan of Generations. It pits Faithful Catholics and all Faithful Christians against their own government. Any and all physical activities not in conformance with God's Plan of Generations and the Nuclear Family are a false, corrupt, and immoral pathway leading one down the road to destruction.

Consubstantial with Jesus Christ, the Holy Spirit is the third person of our One God. Nicodemus had a direct relationship in the flesh with Jesus Christ Himself.

We must take the words of Jesus Christ to Nicodemus—concerning being born again—as the same guidance the Holy Spirit councils for all of us today in our personal consciences.

✝ *What is born of flesh is flesh and what is born of spirit is spirit. Do not be amazed that I told you, 'You must be born from above.' The wind blows where it wills, and you can hear the sound it makes, but you do not know where it comes from or where it goes; so it is with everyone who is born of the Spirit."*
—John 3:6-8
The New American Bible 1987

57

UNITE WITH THE HOLY SPIRIT
AND BE BORN AGAIN

We have the Truth of this throughout the Gospel. For our own spiritual growth and to be Born Again, we must Unite with the Holy Spirit in Truth. We must be public witnesses like Nicodemus in order to defeat all forms of split-consciences and branded/seared consciences which encourage the human mind to cooperate with a fleshly heart on an evil and false path away from Salvation.

JESUS REMINDS THE FAITHFUL
OF A TRUE DISCIPLE

Not everyone who says to me 'Lord, Lord,' will enter the kingdom of heaven, but only the one who does the will of my Father in heaven. Many will say to me on that day, 'Lord, Lord, did we not prophesy in your name? Did we not drive out demons in your name? Did we not do mighty deeds in your name?' Then I will declare to them solemnly, 'I never knew you. Depart from me, you evildoers.'
—Matthew 7:21-23
The New American Bible 1987

FAITH, COURAGE, AND SPIRITUAL
TRANSFORMATION

The Holy Spirit is the only Counselor perfectly integrated with the Faithful Salvation Pathway. One's personal conscience is neither an academic paradigm nor a sophisticated, nuanced decision making process. It is about sincere listening to the Holy Spirit, Faith, courage, understanding the Gospel—including opening to a deeper understanding of Christian doctrines—and the Faithful acts of confession, repentance, and conversion. Yes, a Revolution of Aroused Consciences!

✝ *When the Spirit of truth comes, he will guide you to all truth. He will not speak on his own; but he will speak what he hears, and will declare to you the things that are coming.*
—John 16:13
The New American Bible 1987

JESUS ISSUES STERN
WARNINGS TO HIS DISCIPLES

✝ *"Whoever is not with me is against me, and whoever does not gather with me scatters. Therefore, I say to you, every sin and blasphemy will be forgiven people, but blasphemy against the Spirit will not be forgiven. And whoever speaks a word against the Son of Man will be forgiven, but whoever speaks against the Holy Spirit will not be forgiven, either in this age or in the age to come."*
—Matthew 12:30-32
The New American Bible 1987

As Conscience Warriors aligned with our Almighty God of three persons, we must all rise up, join together, and embrace the power of the living example of Jesus Christ. We must be guided to Salvation by our Counselor, the Holy Spirit; and, peacefully protect our faith, our families, and our precious, innocent children from all of these grave evils.

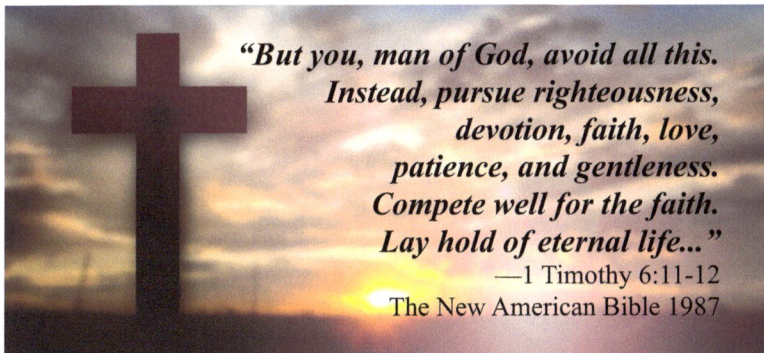

"But you, man of God, avoid all this. Instead, pursue righteousness, devotion, faith, love, patience, and gentleness. Compete well for the faith. Lay hold of eternal life..."
—1 Timothy 6:11-12
The New American Bible 1987

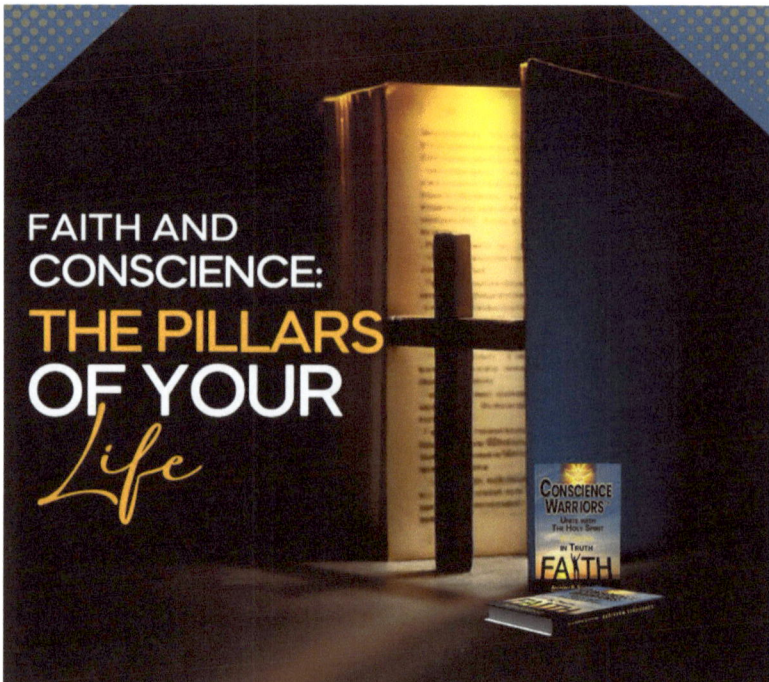

FAITH AND CONSCIENCE: THE PILLARS OF YOUR *Life*

—— X ——

ARCHBISHOP VIGANÒ WARNS FAITHFUL CATHOLICS ABOUT UPCOMING ELECTION

On October 22, 2024, Archbishop Carlo Maria Viganò wrote an Open Letter to American Catholics on the Eve of the 2024 Presidential Election.

Viganò's Open Letter states: "...in this election you must choose between two radically opposed ways of conceiving the government of your Nation: you are called to choose between democracy and dictatorship, between freedom and slavery."

As Conscience Warriors United with The Holy Spirit in Truth, we too know the party that supports abortion through all nine months and beyond and aggressively pushes the LGBTQ+ agenda, is an integral part of the Deep State.

Viganò states that to vote for Harris would be to select "...an infernal monster who obeys Satan." He also asserts that "...we have a candidate and a party that promotes everything that directly opposes the Faith and Morals of the Catholic Church."

Furthermore, Viganò emphasizes that an America under Harris "...is destined for invasion and for moral, social, and economic destruction: the most ferocious dictatorship."

In summarizing his Tuesday letter to American Catholics, Viganò stressed that "...Our Lord must return to reign, and the first way to make Him reign is by obeying His holy law and living in His grace. Let Christ reign in your hearts, in your families, in your communities, and throughout the entire United States of America: this is the only way to peace, harmony, and prosperity for your Nation."

Whoever hammers a lump of iron, first decides what he is going to make of it, a scythe, a sword, or an axe. Even so, we ought to make up our minds what kind of virtue we want to forge or we labour in vain."
—Saint Anthony the Great

Faith, Courage, and Spiritual Transformation

Conscience Warriors have made up our minds what kind of virtue we want to forge and the above quote of St. Anthony contains prophecy to penetrate the Catholic Faithful's crisis of the new millennium and the upcoming 2024 Presidential Election. We invite all Faithful Catholics to read Archbishop Carlo Maria Viganò's October 22, 2024 Open Letter to American Catholics.

Msgr. Carlo Maria Viganò
OPEN LETTER TO AMERICAN CATHOLICS
On The Eve Of The 2024 Presidential Election

The great march of mental destruction will go on.
Everything will be denied. [...]
Fires will be kindled to testify that two and two make four.
Swords will be drawn to prove that leaves are green in summer.
G.K. Chesterton, Heretics, 1905

Dear Faithful American Catholics,

I am addressing all of you, a few days before the Presidential Election that will call millions of American citizens to the polls.

Even in conditions of relative normality, the exercise of the vote is your moral duty, through which you cooperate in the first person in choosing the person who will lead the Nation for the next four years. But in this coming electoral round – just as in 2020 and indeed much more so – you are not simply called to choose between two candidates who happen to be on different political sides but who both nevertheless have the common good at heart in compliance with the Constitution and the Law. No; **in this election you must choose between two radically opposed ways of conceiving the government of your Nation: you are called to choose between democracy and dictatorship, between freedom and slavery.**

On one side we have candidate Donald J. Trump, who, despite serious problems in his positions – especially in the matter of abortion and assisted procreation – has as his objective the common good and the protection of the fundamental freedoms of citizens. In Donald Trump's America, every Catholic can practice their Faith and educate their children in it without interference from the State.

On the other side we have a candidate and a party that promotes everything that directly opposes the Faith and Morals of the Catholic Church. In Kamala Harris' America, Catholics – but also Protestants – are considered fundamentalists to be marginalized and eliminated, and their children are considered the property of the State, which arrogates to itself the right to lead them astray from an early age in both body and soul. Trump's America can become great and prosperous again. Harris' America is destined for invasion and for moral, social, and economic destruction: the most ferocious dictatorship.

Look at your country! Your cities have become dumps filled with derelicts and criminals, drug dealers and addicts, prostitutes and robbers. Your schools are dens of indoctrination and corruption from kindergarten onwards. In your courts, criminals are acquitted and innocents are imprisoned: new ideological crimes are prosecuted, while illegality is tolerated and encouraged. In your hospitals, multinational corporations rule, and you are their guinea pigs to be exterminated or made chronically ill so that you will be their perpetual clients. Farmers, ranchers, and fishermen are persecuted and forced to fail, while the land is grabbed by unscrupulous corporations who transform it into endless photovoltaic systems and wind turbines to power their data centers and server farms where they collect all your data, your movements, your purchases, and your political preferences. They have gone so far as to tamper with the climate by means of sophisticated geoengineering operations and devastating arson in order to make the global warming fraud credible and impose the green transition, the increase in the cost of energy, and electric cars and scooters. And all this is done based on evidence that consists of lies without any scientific proof, but which are propagated through the servile collaboration of the regime media, ever ready to label any dissenters as conspiracy theorists. But what until yesterday was dismissed as the result of conspiracy theories is now admitted by the government itself. They take away your sunlight; they poison you by seeding the clouds; they overwhelm your villages and your fields with deadly hurricanes; they kill your livestock and dry up your crops with induced droughts and devastating fires. They aim to control the entire food sector, to force you to eat only what they make available to you. This is what the Agenda 2030 calls for, which has been imposed without any vote by the United Nations and the World Economic Forum.

In these four disastrous years of the Biden-Harris administration, we have had a puppet in the White House and a corrupt and incompetent Vice President who has never stopped lying and deceiving voters about her past and her future. Power is managed by the criminal deep state – whose names and faces we now know – that is responsible for the destruction of your great Nation. And to ensure that the crisis is endless, new war scenarios are continually opening up, in conflicts that no one actually wants, except for those who make enormous profits from them, sacrificing human lives and compromising international stability.

You have seen what the Democrats, that is, the woke far Left, have been capable of in four years. Imagine what they will be able to do if, instead of Biden's numerous stand-ins, his Vice President is elected – in the most scandalous and unimaginable fraud – with her entourage of LGBTQ+

Ministers, rigorously woke, sold out to China or the World Economic Forum, sponsored by George Soros or Bill Gates, manipulated by Barack Obama and Hillary Clinton. At that point, dear American Catholics, you will not only have to go to a different rally – as Kamala would like – in order to say "Christ is the Lord", because saying that will be considered hate speech, and praying in front of an abortion clinic an act of terrorism. Do not think that these are remote hypotheses: wherever the woke Left takes power, it establishes the most vicious, anti-human, and anti-Christian dictatorship that humanity has ever known. And we know that every time the Left has come to power, it has never left through democratic means.

Donald Trump and Kamala Harris: we are not talking about two visions that are a bit different but still part of the normal political back-and-forth. No; we are talking about two diametrically opposed and irreconcilable worlds, in which Trump fights against the deep state and is committed to freeing America from its tentacled grip, while on the opposite side we have a corrupt and blackmailed candidate, an organic part of the deep state, who acts as a puppet in the hands of warmongers like Barack Obama and Hillary Clinton, of self-proclaimed "philanthropists" like the criminals George Soros and Klaus Schwab, or of characters like Jeffrey Epstein and Sean Combs. Their program is that of the Global Left, the World Economic Forum, the Rockefeller Foundation, the Bill & Melinda Gates Foundation, and ultimately the program of Vanguard, BlackRock, and StateStreet. Their agenda is dictated by the financial oligarchy that controls humanity to the detriment of the people: an elite that operates not only in the United States but also in Canada, Australia, Europe, and wherever politics is held hostage by their investment funds and their pseudo-humanitarian organizations dedicated to the obliteration of Western Civilization.

Behind these people – by now we should know this – are people devoted to evil, united by the satanic hatred against Our Lord Jesus Christ and those who believe in Him, mainly against the Catholic faithful. We want Christ to reign, and we proclaim it with pride: Christ is King! They want the Antichrist to reign, whose tyranny is made of chaos, war, disease, famine, and death. And the more emergencies and crises planned and created by the globalist elite increase, the more that elite has a pretext to impose new limitations, new restrictions of fundamental rights, and new social controls.

Joe Biden, the current "President," is a servant of this subversive elite and widely blackmailable for the scandals and crimes committed by himself personally and also by his family, beginning with his son Hunter. His "Vice President," Kamala Harris, is equally subservient to the same deep state. And the Democratic Party, to which they both belong, is the expression of the woke ideology that plagues all the parties of the global Left.

Candidate Donald J. Trump, while certainly taking some serious critical positions that a Catholic cannot agree with, represents for us, dear American faithful, in this specific historical moment, **the only possible choice to counter the globalist coup that the woke Left is about to implement definitively, irreparably, and with incalculable damage for future generations.**

Voting for Donald Trump means firmly distancing ourselves from an anti-Catholic, anti-Christian and anti-human vision of society. It means stopping those who want to create a hellish dystopia that is even worse than the one announced by George Orwell.

And it also means – do not forget – giving him our vote of confidence, so that President Trump knows that the massive vote of Catholics and Christians that brought him back to the White House **must become the premise for a more incisive commitment to the defense of life from conception to natural death, the traditional family, the right of parents to educate their children, and to the defense of the Christian Faith and the cultural identity of the Nation.**

I repeat: the choice is between a conservative President, who is paying with his very life for his fight against the deep state, and an infernal monster who obeys Satan. For a Catholic, there can be no question: **voting for Kamala Harris is morally inadmissible and constitutes a very grave sin.** Nor is it morally possible to abstain, because **in this war declaring oneself neutral means allying oneself with the enemy.**

People around the world are beginning to understand the threat that looms over them and their children's future, and you Americans have understood it too. But even if this time it will be more difficult for the deep state to repeat the fraud of 2020, you must not think that it will resign itself to defeat so easily. Let us therefore prepare to prevent possible attacks and civil war scenarios from being used to impose martial law and new restrictions, after the attempts on his life from which President Trump providentially escaped.

But let us not forget, dear Faithful, that human energies alone are powerless in the face of this infernal display of forces. We proclaim that Christ is King – this means that Our Lord must return to reign, and the first way to make Him reign is by obeying His holy Law and living in His Grace. Let Christ reign in your hearts, in your families, in your communities, and throughout the entire United States of America: this is the only way to peace, harmony, and prosperity for your Nation.

Think of how many of you Catholics there are in the United States! Vote without hesitation, and pray that Our Lord will enlighten American citizens in making their choice and grant victory to those who, at least, have no problem proclaiming that Christ is Lord.

May God bless you all, and may the Virgin of Guadalupe, she who is the Patroness of the United States and all the Americas, and Saint Michael the Archangel, protect you.

+ Carlo Maria Viganò, *Archbishop, Former Apostolic Nuncio to the United States of America*

October 22, 2024

ARMORED WITH VIRTUE
Conscience Warriors!
TRIUMPH!
www.consciencewarriors.org

—— **XI** ——

FAITHFUL GUARDIANS OF TRUTH— VIGANÒ'S COURAGE TO STAND UP FOR THE TRUTH

Archbishop Carlo Maria Viganò's Open Letter to American Catholics — which he gifted to us prior to the November 5th Presidential election — continues to be a serious wake-up call to all Catholics | Christians.

As we thank God for our Presidential victory on November 5th, we must all continue to arm ourselves with the Conscience Warriors biblical battle plan to help defeat the cultural and sexual indoctrination and grooming which still rages in our schools, hospitals, homes, churches, communities, and nation. As Conscience Warriors, we will tirelessly and unceasingly work to save the hearts and minds of our innocent children and grandchildren, and save the Nuclear Family and God's Plan of Generations from all the related violence and evil.

COURAGE TO STAND UP FOR THE TRUTH

Violence going on around you? Scared to go grocery shopping? Are your close-by gasoline stations becoming shooting zones? What about female Olympic, college, high school, and youth team athletes getting violently attacked by the opposite sex? Violence is just one true cause for personal examinations of conscience! There are many other causes, but let's start with violence.

SEARED & BRANDED CONSCIENCES?

As you know, the definition of "truth" seems to be dramatically changing in this post-truth culture that is infiltrating our homes, schools, communities, and religious institutions. How can any Catholic | Christian safely navigate through all the lies, deceptions, and the "go along to get along" attitudes without actually engaging and examining his or her personal conscience? Or, are consciences readily becoming split, seared, branded, and now collective to the masses?

> *Now the Spirit explicitly says that in the last times some will turn away from the faith by paying attention to deceitful spirits and demonic instructions through the hypocrisy of liars with branded consciences.*
> 1 Timothy 4:1-2
> The New American Bible 1987

✝

> *Now the Spirit manifestly saith that in the last times some shall depart from the faith, giving heed to spirits of error and doctrines of devils. Speaking lies in hypocrisy and having their conscience seared.*
> 1 Timothy 4:1-2
> The Douay Bible 1941

SOUZA HAS ISSUED THE TRUMPET CALL

In *Conscience Warriors, Unite with The Holy Spirit in Truth,* I explore the powerful impact of faith and the unwavering guidance of the Holy Spirit in one's conscience. My narrative is an inspiring beacon that deeply connects with readers worldwide who yearn for ways to fight, peacefully and prayerfully, the corruption and evil going on around them. St. Jude, brother of St. James, speaks openly to those who are called, beloved in God the Father and kept safe for Jesus Christ:

> ✟ *But you, beloved, remember the words spoken beforehand by the apostles of our Lord Jesus Christ, for they told you, "in [the] last time there will be scoffers who will live according to their own godless desires." These are the ones who cause divisions; they live on the natural plane, devoid of the Spirit. But you, beloved, build yourselves up in your most holy faith; pray in the holy Spirit. Keep yourselves in the love of God and wait for the mercy of our Lord Jesus Christ that leads to eternal life.*
> — Jude 1:17-21
> The New American Bible 1987

CONSCIENCE WARRIORS ARM THE FAITHFUL

Conscience Warriors will equip you with an ironclad abundance of Biblical scripture together with saintly writings including those of Saint Pope John Paul II, Saint Augustine, and Saint Anthony. *Conscience Warriors* arms the Faithful with tools to peacefully fight all the violence, lies, and hypocrisy of those individuals who claim to have moral standards and beliefs but their "collective conscience" behavior and actions speak otherwise and do not conform to God's laws and commandments.

> ✟ *Hope has two beautiful daughters; their names are Anger and Courage. Anger at the way things are, and Courage to see that they do not remain as they are.*
> —St. Augustine of Hippo
> The Confessions of St. Augustine

Conscience Warriors are bravely uniting together to fight back against the cultural and political war going on against our innocent children, the Nuclear Family, and all the truths we hold dear. We will not allow those who love the immoral slippery slope of abortion, child sexual abuse, transgenderism, infanticide, critical race and gender theories, LGBTQ++, gay blessings and marriage in the church, to name a few among other "Go Along to Get Along" evils. All this, while ignoring the Christian guidance of confess, repent, and convert.

✝ *Let your prayer be constant, and your conscience pure.*
—Saint Anthony the Great

FAITH, COURAGE, AND SPIRITUAL TRANSFORMATION

Conscience Warriors have made up their minds concerning what kind of virtue they want to forge and the above quote of St. Anthony contains profound prophecy to help penetrate the Catholic Faithful's crisis of the new millennium.

—— **XII** ——

POPE FRANCIS—
AN ERRONEOUS CONSCIENCE
AND ITS ABSENCE OF GUILT

Pope Francis is sheltering himself from the exacting demands of the Truth.

WHAT IS AN ERRONEOUS CONSCIENCE?

Joseph Cardinal Ratzinger—before he was Pope Benedict XVI—advocated truth about the moral conscience with his introduction of Erroneous Conscience in English in 2007 as a critical part of his book *On Conscience*.

The erroneous conscience, by sheltering the person from the exacting demands of truth...appears as subjectivity's protective shell, into which man can escape and there hide from reality.

The obligation to seek the truth terminates, as do any doubts about the general inclination of society and what it has become accustomed to.

The reduction of conscience to subjective certitude betokens at the same time a retreat from truth.

But the departure from truth...now takes its revenge...
which first lulls man into false security and then
abandons him in the trackless waste.
—Joseph Cardinal Ratzinger
On Conscience, 16 & 22

Saint Pope John Paul II also addressed the moral conscience many times and in numerous profound ways with his biblically based writings. All of his writings are based upon the absolute truths of the Christian faith which includes personal guilt as a critical component for the successful work of Salvation guided by the Holy Spirit. It's only in the presence of guilt that one is lead to the Salvation pathway of confession, repentance, and conversion.

...it is always from the truth that the dignity of conscience derives. In the case of the correct conscience, it is a question of the objective truth received by man; in the case of the erroneous conscience, it is a question of what man, mistakenly, subjectively considers to be true.

✝ *Conscience, as the ultimate concrete judgment, compromises its dignity when it is culpably erroneous, that is to say, "when man shows little concern for seeking what is true and good, and conscience gradually becomes almost blind from being accustomed to sin."*
—Saint Pope John Paul II
Veritatis Splendor, Chapter II
Conscience & Truth, 80-81

SHELTERING ONESELF FROM THE EXACTING DEMANDS OF THE TRUTH

Given the criticality of the truth being centric to the development and success of the moral conscience, why then did Pope Francis avoid the truth and remove the Holy Spirit from the moral conscience with his new "moral" conscience incorrectly developed and presented to the world within his Roman Catholic Apostolic Exhortation *Amoris Laetitia* (2016), Chapter 8, 303: pages 234-235?

Here are three condensed quotes of Pope Francis that point out the replacement of the Holy Spirit with the person's pastor as a critical part of the advocated "creative to ideal" conscience:

"…discernment is dynamic…"
"…ever open to new stages of growth…"
"…new decisions which can enable the ideal
to be more fully realized…"

Earlier in time, Cardinal Joseph Ratzinger calls out Pope Francis's currently avoiding the truth with this pronouncement:

We wish to make clear that departure from the church's teaching, or silence about it, in an effort to provide pastoral care is neither caring nor pastoral.
—Joseph Cardinal Ratzinger

In other words, Pope Francis preaches that the person leads God in the conscience which we know is heretical to our beloved Faith! The heretical result is that the absence of guilt interferes with the human Salvation journey.

Often these people fall back on their personal conscience but forget that this conscience is the eye that does not of itself possess light, but only when it looks to the authentic source of light.
—Saint Pope John Paul II
Agenda for the Third Millennium, Evil Chapter, 172

Only the replacement of the moral conscience (which includes guilt) with the "creative to ideal conscience" (absent the Holy Spirit) could then justify and help build a NEW Pope Francis faith. It is a faith that helps promote the Immoral Slippery Slope which now includes the promotion of the LGBTQ+ movement, which further includes the horrors of transgendering children. All of this Erroneous Conscience is further supported by a Split-Conscience™, Branded/Seared Conscience, and Collective Split-Conscience™ as contributory components of a 100% Culpably Erroneous Conscience.

How long will this 100% Erroneous Conscience prevail—with our Church leadership—before our sacred and beloved Church can no longer assist with the Salvation pathway?

✝ ***Here we find ourselves at the very centre of what could be called the 'anti-Word', that is to say the 'anti-Truth'.***
—Saint Pope John Paul II
Agenda for the Third Millennium, Evil Chapter, 141

Conscience Warriors have made up our minds what kind of Faithful virtues we want to forge. These Faithful virtues of course do not include professional nuancing that avoids the truth in some sophisticated way which is corrupting.

✝ *When the Advocate comes whom I will send you from the Father, the Spirit of truth that proceeds from the Father, he will testify to me. And you will also testify, because you have been with me from the beginning.*
—John 15:26-27
The New American Bible 1987

✝ *Only, conduct yourselves in a way worthy of the gospel of Christ, so that,...I may hear news of you, that you are standing firm in one spirit, with one mind struggling together for the faith of the gospel, not intimidated in anyway by your opponents. This is proof to them of destruction, but of your salvation. And this is God's doing. For to you has been granted, for the sake of Christ, not only to believe in him but also to suffer for him.*
—Saint Paul's Letter to the Philippians 1:27-29
The New American Bible 1987

Join with others in being imitators of me, brothers, and observe those who thus conduct themselves according to the model you have in us. For many, as I have often told you and now tell you even in tears, conduct themselves as enemies of the cross of Christ. Their end is destruction. Their God is their stomach; their glory is in their "shame." Their minds are occupied with earthly things. But our citizenship is in heaven, and from it we also await a savior, the Lord Jesus Christ. He will change our lowly body to conform with his glorified body by the power that enables him also to bring all things into subjection to himself.

—Saint Paul's Letter to the Philippians 3:17-21
The New American Bible 1987

—— XIII ——

USCCB MISREPRESENTS THE TRUTH, CHAMPIONS ILLEGAL ALIENS, AND ABANDONS MAINTAINING ABORTION AS ITS *PREEMINENT PRIORITY*

Our American "Catholic Leaders" — USCCB

What role does philosophical thought play in the USCCB's ongoing actions that ultimately abandon its recent vote (225-11) to maintain Abortion as their Preeminent Priority?

Could the "professional" use of philosophy—when it promulgates that a human being is equal in any way to the three Divine persons of The Holy Trinity—be the foundation for the intellectual nuancing that defeats the holy communion with God that assists the human conscience to function properly?

According to Michael Hichborn, President of the Lepanto Institute — www.lepantoin.org:

"...the USCCB does next to nothing to combat the murder of preborn children, while spending gobs of cash facilitating the resettlement of people entering this country illegally."

Further statistics referenced by Mr. Hichborn reveal that:

"...financial reports for 2022 and 2023 don't even mention the pro-life activities office, but they do show that the budget for Migration and Refugee services jumped to $127 million and $134 million, respectively."

"...up from $82 million in 2017. Pro-life activities office average budget of $2.164 million for period 2014-2021."

The USCCB's splitting of words and actions is heretical to our beloved Faith as it opposes God's Plan of Generations while ignoring the Divine inseparability of our Trinitarian Family: God the Father, God the Son, and their Holy Spirit.

> ✝ *For the love of money is the root of all evils, and some people in their desire for it have strayed from the faith and have pierced themselves with many pains.*
> —1 Timothy 6:10
> The New American Bible 1987

PHILOSOPHY VS. THEOLOGY

The USCCB is using philosophical thought that is completely and solely dependent on human nuancing for its persuasion power. Their philosophy vs. theology eats away at the blessed communion between God and man with the production of extremely erroneous and hypocritical guidance for the human conscience that misleads the Salvation pathway.

Protecting the unborn is no way comparable to those that intentionally break the law to force entry into a country that has a successful operating system to assist those seeking asylum and the legitimate related.

✝ *Knowing their malice, Jesus said, "Why are you testing me, you hypocrites? Show me the coin that pays the census tax." Then they handed him the Roman coin. He said to them, "Whose image is this and whose inscription?" They replied, "Caesar's." At that he said to them, "Then repay to Caesar what belongs to Caesar and to God what belongs to God." When they heard this they were amazed, and leaving him they went away.*
—Matthew 22:18-22
The New American Bible 1987

Those individuals who intentionally break the law that provides controlled safety for all citizens cannot expect to be USA citizens. For the USCCB to assist such immoral expectation by aiding and abetting with their law breaking endeavor—as they choose to misrepresent the truth of their abortion preeminent priority—is the abandonment of the clergy's vows and cannot be corrected with a gaslighting campaign full of lies. Lies developed by the USCCB leadership to convince citizens that the unborn are not as important to protect as are illegal aliens that intentionally break the law—including a high percentage of very dangerous criminals—are an utter rejection of the Holy Trinity.

MODERN DAY MONEY CHANGERS

Today's money changers—including the USCCB—are aided and abetted by a widespread, postmodern day sociology and philosophy, that derail moral theology after being corrupted by a deep paradigm driven by the pursuit of money, power, and glory.

✝ *Jesus entered the temple area and drove out all those engaged in selling and buying there. He overturned the tables of the money changers and the seats of those who were selling doves. And he said to them, "it is written:*

✝

'My house shall be a house of prayer,'
but you are making it a den of thieves.
—Matthew 21:12-13
The New American Bible 1987

No one can serve two masters.
He will either hate one and love the other,
or be devoted to one, and despise the other.
You cannot serve God and mammon.
—Matthew 6:24
The New American Bible 1987

To further emphasize the USCCB's obvious love of money, power, and glory, in his Open Letter to American Catholics dated 02/02/2025, Archbishop Carlo Maria Viganò states:

"It is no mystery that the United States Conference of Catholic Bishops (USCCB) has never —and I repeat: never — raised a penny to fight abortion, but rather has funded with tens of millions of dollars associations that adhere to the Catholic Campaign for Human Development and promote abortion, contraception, and homosexuality. Nor does the USCCB have any qualms about receiving subsidies from the Department of the Treasury for its management of illegal immigration, as its budgets, which are public, prove. And it should be remembered that, in addition to government funds, the USCCB receives funding from institutions and private foundations for the same purposes."

THE HYPOSTATIC UNION

The Hypostatic Union—the always perfect, simultaneous, and continuous combining of Jesus Christ's two perfect and infallible natures of Divine & human as an integral part of the Holy Trinity—is the combination of Jesus' Divine & human natures that help empower man to understand the correct Salvation pathway as counseled by The Holy Spirit. Christ used his freedom perfectly, humans do not. To be saved, we must always avoid any thinking whatsoever that compares our human selves with Almighty God in any way. God is the only Almighty. Humans are sinners that absolutely need the grace of God to be saved. The USCCB is putting solely human reasoned and highly nuanced philosophical thought ahead of and in place of the absolute truth.

As you know, the definition of "truth" seems to be dramatically changing in this post-truth culture that is infiltrating our homes, schools, communities, and religious institutions. How can any Catholic | Christian safely navigate through all the lies, deceptions, and the "Go Along to Get Along" attitudes without actually engaging and examining his or her personal conscience with the help of the Holy Spirit.

> ✝ *I speak the truth in Christ, I do not lie; my conscience joins with the Holy Spirit in bearing me witness...*
> —Romans 9:1
> The New American Bible 1987

CONSCIENCE WARRIORS ARM THE FAITHFUL

Conscience Warriors will equip you with an ironclad abundance of Biblical Scripture together with saintly writings including those of Saint Pope John Paul II, Saint Augustine, and Saint Anthony.

Conscience Warriors arms the Faithful with tools to peacefully fight all the violence, lies, and hypocrisy of those individuals who claim to have Faithful moral standards and beliefs but their Collective Conscience behavior and actions speak otherwise and do not conform to God's laws and commandments.

✝ *God has promised forgiveness to your repentance, but He has not promised tomorrow to your procrastination. Put no faith in salvation through the political order. The cost of obedience is small compared with the cost of disobedience.*

—St. Augustine of Hippo

FAITH, COURAGE, & SPIRITUAL TRANSFORMATION

Conscience Warriors are bravely uniting together to fight back against the cultural and political war going on against our innocent children, the Nuclear Family, and all the truths we hold dear. We will not allow those who love the immoral slippery slope of abortion, child sexual abuse, transgenderism, infanticide, critical race and gender theories, LGBTQ++, gay blessings and marriage in the church, to name a few among other "Go Along to Get Along" evils. All this, while ignoring the Christian guidance of confess, repent, and convert.

SOUZA HAS ISSUED THE TRUMPET CALL

Prolife Leader Frank Pavone, National Director, Priests for Life; and President, National Pro-life Religious Council shares his endorsement for *Conscience Warriors*:

Our enemies today rebel against God's truth – denying that a man is a man, a woman is a woman, and a baby is a baby. They likewise rebel against freedom, seeking to force our conscience to bow to their tyranny. Anthony Souza has issued the trumpet call we all need in Conscience Warriors. To be true to God and to ourselves, we must, in conscience, speak the truth and act in freedom, no matter what the cost.

— Frank Pavone
National Director, Priests for Life

—— XIV ——

CONSCIENCE WARRIORS EXAMINE THE CHURCH'S INTEGRITY — WILL THE NEXT PAPAL CONCLAVE MIRROR THE LAST ONE?

What is the Underlying Reason for Pope Benedict XVI's Resignation and/or Retirement Back in 2013?

On February 20, 2025 *LifeSite News* published the following opinion by—

John-Henry Westen, Co-Founder, CEO,
Editor of *LifeSite* News
Michael Matt, Editor of the *Remnant*
Elizabeth Yore, *Yore Children*
David L. Sonnier, LTC US Army (Ret.)

"Shortly after the first inauguration of President Trump in 2017, an open letter was published in The Remnant Newspaper requesting an investigation into potential involvement by the...Administration in the affairs of the Catholic Church. Specifically, the authors asked whether the U.S. Government was involved in the sequence of events that resulted in the resignation of Pope Benedict XVI on February 11, 2013 and the Conclave that elected Pope Francis on March 13, 2013. This open letter was widely circulated throughout the world, but no action was taken during the first Trump administration. Consequently, the questions that were raised remain unanswered."[1]

"We are asking for an investigation into the affairs of our own government. It is not unprecedented for a corrupt government to attempt to insert itself into the life of the Church."[1]

Questions in this open letter included the following bullets; however, more are in the actual article and we are simply referencing 4 of the questions to help identify the truth about the efforts of our government to move our beloved Church towards a new World Order that is built upon destroying the good and empowering evil.

• What other covert operations were carried out by U.S. government operatives concerning the resignation of Pope Benedict or the conclave that elected Pope Francis?[1]

• To what end was the National Security Agency monitoring the conclave that elected Pope Francis?[1]

• International monetary transactions with the Vatican were suspended during the last few days prior to the resignation of Pope Benedict. Were any U.S. Government agencies involved in this?[1]

• Why were international monetary transactions resumed on February 12, 2013, the day after Benedict XVI announced his resignation? Was this pure coincidence?[1]

CONSCIENCE WARRIORS
ARE FAITHFUL GUARDIANS OF TRUTH

Given what Conscience Warriors know today about the overwhelming lies, fraud, and money laundering embedded in our government as its Deep State individuals seek money, power, and glory with the will to do just about anything and everything to hide their evil deeds from justice and remain in power. Our personal consciences must not only be United with The Holy Spirit in Truth concerning our personal Pathway to Salvation, our consciences must also seek the truth concerning any "Go Along to Get Along" behavior in our Church today that is aligned with the new World Order.

THE CHURCH'S "CREATIVE TO THE IDEAL" CONSCIENCE EVAPORATES INTELLECTUAL INTEGRITY!

Pope Francis' release of his Apostolic Exhortation *Amoris Laetitia's* (2016) with its heretical Chapter 8, pages 233-235, and directly in paragraphs 302 & 303, concerning a new, human idea that a "creative to the ideal" conscience is in reference to the evolving of the "objective ideal". The Holy Spirit is displaced by pastors and priests in the human conscience all of which is outside the overall demands of the Gospel.

A "creative to the ideal" conscience evaporates intellectual integrity by living "according to the flesh" which demands flexibility of conscience to convince oneself that human logic alone must prevail with decision making. In other words, the person is unable to sustain intellectual integrity which is evaporated by the heat of an emotionally-centric manipulation of the Faithful synthesis of conscience, heart, and mind as he/she morphs into a "self-styled" Catholic/Christian further empowering "situation ethics".

If in fact—yet to be completely verified as stated in the first paragraph above—U.S. Government officials helped to force Pope Benedict's resignation, the release of *Amoris Laetitia* in 2016—in direct opposition to Joseph Cardinal Ratzinger's book *On Conscience*—cannot be a coincidence. It would have had to be planned, crafted, and carried out to assist the new World Order.

Further, *Amoris Laetitia's* Chapter 8 is in direct opposition to Pope Benedict's book *On Conscience* which develops Erroneous Conscience.

Archbishop Carlo Maria Viganò* expressed in *Vitium Consensus* in October of 2023:
We know that ...the globalist elite in general...was supposed to oust Benedict XVI from the papacy, elect an ultra progressive pope, and substantially modify the Catholic Magisterium by making it accept the demands of the Agenda 2030: gender equality, the introduction of gender ideology and LGBTQ+ doctrine, the democratization of Church governance, collaboration in the neo-Malthusian project of the Great Reset, cooperation on immigrationism, and cancel culture.[2]

Archbishop Viganò continues:
The consensus and support for the Argentine Jesuit comes significantly from the ultra-progressive and pro-heretical wing that sponsored his election: all notorious members of the deep church and closely-linked to the homosexual and pedophile lobby of the deep state.[2]

WHY ARE CONSCIENCE WARRIORS CALLING ALL OF THIS OUT?

We must examine not only our own consciences, we must fully examine the Erroneous Conscience of the Church—Joseph Cardinal Ratzinger wrote about in *On Conscience*—that can move us off the Faithful Salvation pathway.

Conscience Warriors, United with The Holy Spirit in Truth, know that the church in Rome has supported and continues to aggressively push the woke, LGBTQ+ agenda which is an alignment of sorts involving the Deep State and the Deep Church.

> *A time is coming when men will go mad, and when they see someone who is not mad, they will attack him saying, 'You are mad; you are not like us.'*
> —Saint Anthony the Great

Conscience Warriors have made up our minds what kind of virtue we want to forge and the above quote of St. Anthony contains prophecy to help penetrate the Catholic Faithful's crisis of the new millennium, and the challenges faced by true seekers of spiritual truth.

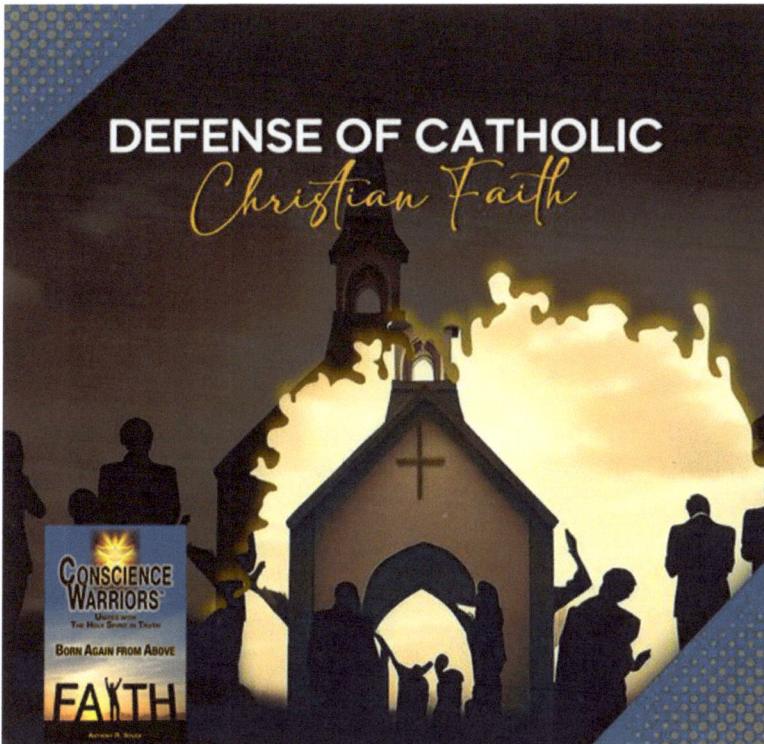

TRANSFORMATION —
OUR FIRST CONSCIENCE WARRIORS

Saint Joseph of Arimathea, a distinguished member of the council of his time, courageously and successfully "broke out" and away from the "Go Along to Get Along" and Collective Split-Conscience™ of his religious leadership—the Scribes, Pharisees, and Sadducees—and demonstrated the first and corrective step that our Salvation pathway demands. He integrated his words and actions. He asked Pilate for Jesus' body and he used his own tomb for Jesus' burial.

Did Joseph examine his own conscience together with the obvious Erroneous Consciences of his leadership? Had to be. We need to follow in the footsteps of Joseph of Arimathea— Our First Conscience Warrior!

Saint Nicodemus — Our Second Conscience Warrior. He too, along with Joseph of Arimathea, was in high position with the Jews and a rich and religious man. He was led by the truth to go to Jesus at night. Nicodemus believed his eyes and ears. Jesus was aware of Nicodemus' good faith efforts and schooled him on being Born Again.

In the First Letter of Peter, Peter also schools others on integrating words and actions to be born anew:

Since you have purified yourselves by obedience to the truth for sincere mutual love, love one another intensely from a [pure] heart. You have been born anew, not from perishable but from imperishable seed, through the living and abiding word of God...
—1 Peter 1:22-23
The New American Bible

Our human consciences and the Collective Conscience of the Church must be filled with the Holy Spirit. The Holy Spirit cannot be squeezed out by many in our Church leadership whose consciences are aligned with the Deep State and its new World Order, "self-styled" religion, and the "creative" to the "ideal" — which is at the heart of all this Faith deterioration by nefarious hypocrites and money changers — all feeding off of radical feminism and its immoral slippery slope.

> *Children, let us love not in word or*
> *speech but in deed and truth.*
> —1 John 3:18
> The New American Bible

✞

> *But if you warn the wicked man, trying to turn him from*
> *his way, and he refuses to turn from his way, he shall die*
> *for his guilt, but you shall save yourself.*
> —Ezekiel 33:9
> The New American Bible

---

1. *LifeSite News* link to: RemnantNewspaper.com/web/index.php/articles/item/3001-did-vatican-attempt-to-influence-u-s-election-catholics-ask-trump-administration-to-investigate

2. Archbishop Carlo Maria Viganò, Former Apostolic Nuncio to the United States of America

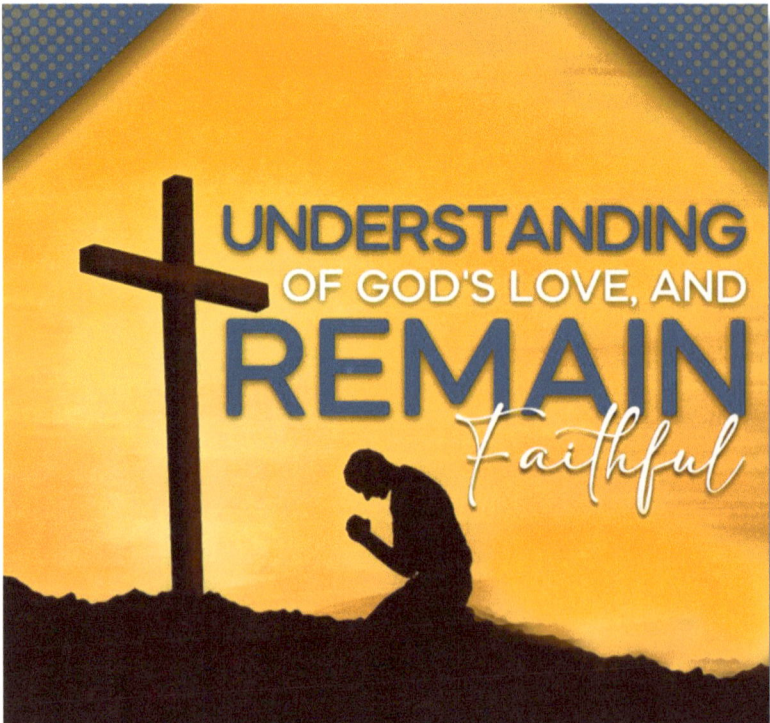
UNDERSTANDING OF GOD'S LOVE, AND REMAIN Faithful

—— CONCLUSION ——

THAT WHICH THE SPIRIT WILLS
INTEGRATION OF HEART, MIND, AND CONSCIENCE

Inspired by the *Born Again From Above* Conscience Warriors, Saint Joseph of Arimathea and Saint Nicodemus, we embrace, covet, and promote all Biblical truths which have at their core the "triunity of God for the moral life of man...just as the divine persons are inseparable and coinherent, man is called to a coinherence of words and actions, faith and life."[1]

As were Saints Joseph of Arimathea and Nicodemus, we are leaders also as Conscience Warriors with Divine help to—as we follow Jesus' life example—recognize and condemn the lies, deceitful acts, and hypocrisy of the Deep State and the Deep Church.

Schooled directly by Jesus about the pathway to Salvation, Nicodemus was able to integrate his **heart, mind, and conscience** to synthesize the **intellectual integrity** that he desperately needed to successfully proceed on his spiritual journey for Salvation.

---

1. Dr. Adrian Walker, Professor of Philosophy and Dogmatics, St. Patrick's Seminary.

Nicodemus became Born Again in the image and likeness of Jesus Christ by embracing truth and breaking out from the "Go Along to Get Along" prevailing paradigm of the leaders of his times.

We too must be particularly aware of the sins of groupthink, brainwashing, gaslighting, indoctrinating/programming, and any/all sinful human behavior, so as to be able to respond in Truth to questions and evil actions of those—like the leaders of Nicodemus' times—with "Go Along to Get Along" personal paradigms and/or "Creative to the Ideal" consciences that feed their stubborn sinful behavior.

✚
> *To the clean all things are clean, but to those who are defiled and unbelieving nothing is clean; in fact, both their minds and their consciences are tainted. They claim to know God, but by their deeds they deny him. They are vile and disobedient and unqualified for any good deed.*
> —Titus 1:15
> The New American Bible

As we begin the journey of being **Born Again From Above**, let us always remember that Jesus, consubstantial with the Father and on Pentecost, sent the Holy Spirit to be with all of us as Counselor in our personal consciences and a Divine guide for Salvation.

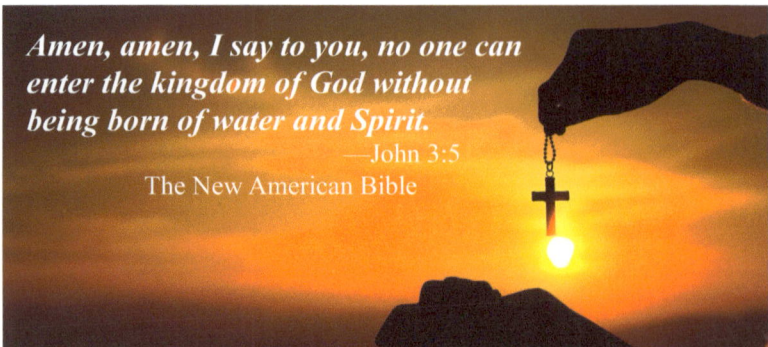

Amen, amen, I say to you, no one can enter the kingdom of God without being born of water and Spirit.
—John 3:5
The New American Bible

CONSCIENCE WARRIORS™
UNITE WITH THE HOLY SPIRIT IN TRUTH
ENDORSEMENTS & TESTIMONIALS • 1st Edition

"Our enemies today rebel against God's truth — denying that a man is a man, a woman is a woman, and a baby is a baby. They likewise rebel against freedom, seeking to force our conscience to bow to their tyranny. Anthony Souza has issued the trumpet call we all need in Conscience Warriors. To be true to God and to ourselves, we must, in conscience, speak the truth and act in freedom, no matter what the cost."
> —Prolife Leader Frank Pavone, National Director
> Priests for Life President, National Pro-life Religious Council

"Contemporary Western culture understands freedom simply as the ability to act on one's own initiative, detached from any underlying ground or orienting purpose. As Mr. Souza sees, what is needed is a return to a traditional understanding of conscience, which is nothing other than the voice of Christ — every person's true Ground and Goal — present in our soul, enabling us to fulfill our supernatural destiny and thus be truly free. This book is a timely reminder that the Truth of Christ and the Freedom of Man are one."   —Michael Presberg, Ph.D. Candidate
> Pontifical John Paul II Institute for Studies on Marriage & Family

"In his timely and provocative book, Anthony Souza identifies the most critical issue of our time, the collapse of conscience. Souza urgently calls on all Catholics Christians to become Conscience Warriors and to refocus on the Gospel mandate to repent, turn away from sin, and follow Jesus. This book will save souls!"   —Francis D. Dezelski, M.T.S.
> Pontifical John Paul II Institute for Studies on Marriage & Family

"This book offers a powerful reflection of what happens when we chose to remain silent about issues that our conscience reveals are evil. Souza identifies how a "split-conscience" allows good people to agree they would not choose to do something that is evil, but at the same time they allow others the opportunity to act in evil ways. Clearly this indicates a lack of love for God and our neighbor. We are called to be "Conscience Warriors" in this world. Souza points out the wonderful gift of the Holy Spirit has been given to everyone. It is our Christian duty to help spread the Light of God's Truth to those who lack understanding and this book helps us identify some areas that need illumination."
> —Thomas H. & Laura Jones, The Dignity Mandate, Inc.

"I learned much from this compelling book on the serious threats Western Culture and the Catholic Church are facing which are threatening their very survival. Souza talks about how the Nuclear Family is under constant attack from false ideologies such as Transgenderism and Radical Feminism. But all is not gloom as he tells us how we can take back Our Faith, Our Families, Our Churches, Our Schools, Our Republic, and Our World."   —Jack Ames, P.E., Founder DEFEND LIFE

"Morality and personal faith are under tremendous and constant assault. Counter culturalism, new age thinking, wokeism, radical feminism, and simple relaxed moral thinking are among the many threats to traditional moral & religious values. The pressure placed on young and old alike is constant and unyielding. Left unchecked, it is easy to see how a person's personal values and religious convictions can be gradually and insidiously degraded by a "Go Along to Get Along" group mentality. This is why I found *Conscience Warriors* an important book for our times. The author, Anthony Souza, identifies the threats and challenges confronted by people of all faiths and conscience. He exposes the ploys and false premises being extolled as "today thinking" and offers faith-based solutions and counter strategies to defeat them. I found Anthony's book a timely and meaningful read and heartily recommend it to others."
—John Paraschak, Knights of Columbus Council #1384

"Thank you, Anthony, for undertaking the important work of unfolding the implications of the triunity of God for the moral life of man. I'm in deep accord with your fundamental intuition: just as the divine persons are inseparable and coinherent, man is called to a coinherence of words and actions, faith and life. This coinherence— and the unity and integrity of conscience it enables — is crucial to the fulfillment of man's vocation to participate in the intra-trinitarian life."
—Dr. Adrian Walker, Ph.D.
Professor of Philosophy and Dogmatics, St. Patrick's Seminary

International Impact Book Awards Winner Christian, Non-Fiction December 2024

2024 INTERNATIONAL IMPACT BOOK AWARDS
- WINNER -
AWARDED TO
Anthony R. Souza, M.T.S.
Conscience Warriors: Unite with The Holy Spirit in Truth
Christian - Christian Non-Fiction

Author **Anthony R. Souza** is the Owner of Souza Development and The Souza Agency, Inc., and Past President & CEO of Pro-Life MD. A graduate of the United States Coast Guard Academy, he served six years on active duty, which included four years at sea and a two-year, sea-going, search & rescue command.

Anthony has worked tirelessly to build his entire entrepreneurial and spirited career around marriage and family, helping and inspiring individuals to make sound and secure decisions for their future in communion with the Holy Spirit. Anthony's Master of Theological Studies (M.T.S.) advanced degree in Marriage and Family from the Pontifical John Paul II Institute at the Catholic University of America guided his speaking engagements on Marriage and Family and Catholic Social Teaching. These speaking engagements included St. Thomas More Lecture Series, the Knights of Columbus/Catholic Information Center, Theology on Tap, and Adult Faith Enrichment classes at St. Mary's Parish in Annapolis. Topics included Father & Son: The Trinitarian Relationship in the Flesh; Confrontation to Communion: Conversion for Innocent Human Life; Marriage & God's Plan of Generations: The Salvation Opportunity, Communion Inside Gift of Self, Human Sexuality & Parenting, Sexuality/Unitive & Procreative; Conscience & Communion: Linking the Heart with Action.

Anthony and his wife, Roseanne, are blessed with two wonderful and loving Sons and "Daughters", and seven Grandsons.

"...Most of all, thanks for your constant vigorous and courageous defense of those truths and values that stand at the heart of the Gospel and human civilization."   —Dr. David Schindler, Dean Emeritus
Pontifical John Paul II Institute for Studies on Marriage & Family

CONSCIENCE WARRIORS™

UNITE WITH
THE HOLY SPIRIT IN TRUTH

BORN AGAIN FROM ABOVE

ANTHONY R. SOUZA